Planning on the Edge

Jaydan Tait

Planning on the Edge

Policy Recommendations Addressing Problematic Residential Industrial District Interfaces

VDM Verlag Dr. Müller

Imprint

Bibliographic information by the German National Library: The German National Library lists this publication at the German National Bibliography; detailed bibliographic information is available on the Internet at
http://dnb.d-nb.de.

Any brand names and product names mentioned in this book are subject to trademark, brand or patent protection and are trademarks or registered trademarks of their respective holders. The use of brand names, product names, common names, trade names, product descriptions etc. even without a particular marking in this works is in no way to be construed to mean that such names may be regarded as unrestricted in respect of trademark and brand protection legislation and could thus be used by anyone.

Cover image: www.purestockx.com

Published 2008 Saarbrücken

Publisher:
VDM Verlag Dr. Müller Aktiengesellschaft & Co. KG , Dudweiler Landstr. 125 a,
66123 Saarbrücken, Germany,
Phone +49 681 9100-698, Fax +49 681 9100-988,
Email: info@vdm-verlag.de

Produced in Germany by:
Reha GmbH, Dudweilerstrasse 72, D-66111 Saarbrücken
Schaltungsdienst Lange o.H.G., Zehrensdorfer Str. 11, 12277 Berlin, Germany
Books on Demand GmbH, Gutenbergring 53, 22848 Norderstedt, Germany

Impressum

Bibliografische Information der Deutschen Nationalbibliothek: Die Deutsche Nationalbibliothek verzeichnet diese Publikation in der Deutschen Nationalbibliografie; detaillierte bibliografische Daten sind im Internet über http://dnb.d-nb.de abrufbar.

Alle in diesem Buch genannten Marken und Produktnamen unterliegen warenzeichen-, marken- oder patentrechtlichem Schutz bzw. sind Warenzeichen oder eingetragene Warenzeichen der jeweiligen Inhaber. Die Wiedergabe von Marken, Produktnamen, Gebrauchsnamen, Handelsnamen, Warenbezeichnungen u.s.w. in diesem Werk berechtigt auch ohne besondere Kennzeichnung nicht zu der Annahme, dass solche Namen im Sinne der Warenzeichen- und Markenschutzgesetzgebung als frei zu betrachten wären und daher von jedermann benutzt werden dürften.

Coverbild: www.purestockx.com

Erscheinungsjahr: 2008
Erscheinungsort: Saarbrücken

Verlag: VDM Verlag Dr. Müller Aktiengesellschaft & Co. KG , Dudweiler Landstr. 125 a,
D- 66123 Saarbrücken,
Telefon +49 681 9100-698, Telefax +49 681 9100-988,
Email: info@vdm-verlag.de

Herstellung in Deutschland:
Schaltungsdienst Lange o.H.G., Zehrensdorfer Str. 11, D-12277 Berlin
Books on Demand GmbH, Gutenbergring 53, D-22848 Norderstedt
Reha GmbH, Dudweilerstrasse 72, D-66111 Saarbrücken

ISBN: 978-3-639-01377-1

Abstract

Planning on the Edge: Policy Recommendations Addressing Problematic Residential-Industrial District Interfaces

Student's Name: **Jaydan Dean Tait**

Date: **August 30, 2002**

Prepared in partial fulfillment of the requirements of the degree in the Faculty of Environmental Design, the University of Calgary.

Supervisors' Names: **Dr. Stanley M. Stein, Diane Hooper, M.E.Des**

Areas in cities exist where residential and industrial land uses border one another. The location of these incompatible land uses have resulted both from settlement patterns that predate zoning practices and calculated placement of these areas next to one another. At these interfaces, the activities of the adjacent land uses can produce negative externalities that adversely affect the neighbouring district. The citywide policies of Calgary and other Canadian municipalities were reviewed to determine how land use policies address the management of these interface areas. The various conditions produced at problematic interfaces were catalogued and the residential-industrial interface areas of Calgary were categorized to identify the most problematic areas in the City. Planners responsible for the creation of Area Redevelopment Plans (ARPs) at identified problematic interfaces were interviewed to rate the success of localized planning interventions. The results of the citywide policy reviews, the planner interviews, ARP reviews, and field excursions were collected to develop policy recommendations outlining various ways Calgary can better manage problematic interface areas and minimize the effects of existing negative conditions.

Key Words:

Industrial Planning
Land Use Interface
Negative Externality
Performance Standards
Planning Policy
Zoning

Table of Contents

Approval Page...i
Abstract..ii
Title Page...iii
Acknowledgments...iv
Table of Contents..v
List of Figure and Tables..ix

Chapter 1- Industrial Land Use Planning in Canada and Calgary
   1.1- Introduction..1
   1.2- The Origins of Land Use Planning..................................3
   1.3- Europe; The Crucible of Organized Land Use Planning........4
   1.4- Industrial Land Use Planning in North America..................6
   1.5- The Early Industrial History of Calgary............................8
   1.6- Industrial Land Use Districts..11
   1.7- Calgary Policy Concerning Residential-Industrial Interfaces....12
      1.7.1- The Calgary Plan..13
      1.7.2- The Calgary Land Use Bylaw................................14
   1.8- Conclusion...18

Chapter 2- Interface Land Use Policy in Canadian Municipalities
   2.1- Introduction..21
   2.2- Canadian Municipal Industrial Interface Policy.................22
      2.2.1- Edmonton..22
         2.2.1.1- Plan Edmonton: Edmonton's Municipal Development Plan.............22
         2.2.1.2- Edmonton Zoning Bylaw 2001..23
      2.2.2- Hamilton...26
         2.2.2.1- Hamilton Zoning Bylaw 1980..26
      2.2.3- Ottawa..26
         2.2.3.1- Ottawa Regional Plan 1999..26
         2.2.3.2- City of Ottawa Official Plan 1994..27
      2.2.4- Regina...28
         2.2.4.1- Regina Development Plan..28
         2.2.4.2- Regina Zoning Bylaw 1992..28
      2.2.5- Saskatoon..31
         2.2.5.1- Saskatoon Development Plan 1998..31
         2.2.5.2- Saskatoon Zoning Bylaw No. 6772, 1987................................31
         2.2.5.3- Municipal Enterprise Zones in Saskatoon, 2002 Discussion Paper... 32
      2.2.6- Toronto...33
         2.2.6.1- Toronto Official Plan Part 1, 1987..33
         2.2.6.2- Toronto Official Plan Summary, 2002.....................................33
      2.2.7- Vancouver..34
         2.2.7.1- Vancouver CityPlan, 1995...34
         2.2.7.2- Vancouver Zoning and Development Bylaw No. 3575...................34

Table of Contents

    2.2.8- Victoria..37
        2.2.8.1- Victoria Official Regional Plan 1974..37
        2.2.8.2- Victoria Zoning Bylaw 1999..38
    2.2.9- Winnipeg..39
        2.2.9.1- Plan Winnipeg 2001..39
        2.2.9.2- Winnipeg Zoning By-law..40
2.3- Canadian Residential-Industrial Interface Policy Matrix.........41
2.4- Conclusion...42

Chapter 3- Problematic Residential-Industrial Interfaces
3.1- What is a Problematic Interface?......................................45
3.2- The Problematic Phenomena at the Interface.....................46
    3.2.1- Air Pollution...47
    3.2.2- Blast Overpressure..48
    3.2.3- Broadcast (Electrical) Interference....................................48
    3.2.4- Effluent...48
    3.2.5- Fire and Explosive Hazards...48
    3.2.6- Glare...49
    3.2.7- Heat and Humidity..49
    3.2.8- Litter..49
    3.2.9- Noise..50
    3.2.10- Odour...50
    3.2.11- On Street Parking...50
    3.2.12- Outdoor Storage and Waste Disposal.............................51
    3.2.13- Particulate Matter...51
    3.2.14- Radiation Emissions..51
    3.2.15- Toxic and Hazardous Materials.....................................52
    3.2.16- Traffic...52
    3.2.17- Undesirable Social Activity..52
    3.2.18- Unsightly Properties...53
    3.2.19- Vibration...53
    3.2.20- Water Quality Deterioration...53
    3.2.21- Lodging Unmerited Complaints....................................54
    3.2.22- On Street Parking...54
    3.2.23- Shortcutting through Industrial Districts........................54
3.3- Groupings of Negative Externalities................................55
    3.3.1- Group 1: High Risk Negative Externalities........................55
    3.3.2- Group 2: Nuisance-Only Negative Externalities.................55
3.4- The Industrial Areas of Calgary......................................56
3.5- Residential-Industrial Interfaces in Calgary by Community....58
3.6- Interface Conditions by Residential Community.................59
    3.6.1- Water Feature..59
    3.6.2- Transportation Route..59
    3.6.3- Berm..60
    3.6.4- Fence...60
    3.6.5- Park of Open Space..60

3.6.6- Another Land Use District.. 60
3.7- Towards a Typology of Problematic Interfaces................... 62
    3.7.1- Residences within 200 metres of Industrial Land.................... 63
    3.7.2- The Quality of the Interface Condition................................. 64
    3.7.3- Incidents of Reported Problems by City of Calgary Staff........... 65
3.8- The Problematic Residential-Industrial Interface Typology..... 65
    3.8.1- Category 1: Non-Problematic Residential-Industrial Interfaces... 65
    3.8.2- Category 2: Nuisance Only Residential-Industrial Interfaces...... 66
    3.8.3- Category 3: The Most Problematic Interfaces........................ 66
3.9- Conclusion..67

Chapter 4- Interface Policy Created for Calgary Communities
4.1- Introduction.. 71
4.2- What is and Area Redevelopment Plan?........................... 72
4.3- ARP Reviews and Interview Results................................. 73
    4.3.1- Forest Lawn-Forest Heights/Hubalta ARP...........................73
    4.3.2- Inglewood ARP...75
    4.3.3- Manchester ARP...78
    4.3.4- Millican-Ogden Community Revitalization Plan................... 79
    4.3.5- Ramsay ARP.. 82
4.4- Ongoing Problematic Interface Areas............................... 83
    4.4.1- Fairview... 83
    4.4.2- Highland Park.. 85
4.5- ARP Industrial Interface Policy Comparison..................... 87
4.6- Conclusion.. 88

Chapter 5- Options for Calgary Interfaces
5.1- Introduction... 91
5.2- The Range of Options... 91
    5.2.1- Continued Use of Existing Policy...................................... 92
    5.2.2- New Style Community Planning.. 93
    5.2.3- Performance Based Industrial Land Use Planning................. 93
    5.2.4- Risk Based Land Use Planning.. 94
    5.2.5- Land Use Bylaw Rewrite... 97
        5.2.5.1- Transitional Business District... 97
        5.2.5.2-Live-Work Transition District.. 97
        5.2.5.3- Traditional Industrial District... 99
    5.2.6- Industrial Interface Redevelopment Guidelines..................... 100
    5.2.7- Visual Screening and Buffering Requirements...................... 100
    5.2.8- Industrial Area BRZ.. 101
5.3- Interface Policy Options and the Calgary Context................ 101
5.4- Conclusion..103

Table of Contents

Chapter 6- The Residential-Industrial Interface Policy
6.1- The Need for a New Industrial Interface District.................. 107
6.2- General Rules for Industrial Districts................................108
6.3- IR Light Industrial-Residential Interface District................. 111
6.4- Conclusions... 115
6.5- Planning Over the Edge: Ongoing Research Possibilities....... 116

Appendices
Appendix A- Zoning and Development Control in the City of Calgary......119
Appendix B- Edmonton Industrial Interface Policy............................ 120
Appendix C- Sound Levels and Human Response............................. 122
Appendix D- Hamilton Industrial Interface Policy.............................124
Appendix E- Ottawa Industrial Interface Policy.................................125
Appendix F- Regina Industrial Interface Policy................................. 127
Appendix G- Saskatoon Industrial Interface Policy............................ 128
Appendix H- Toronto Industrial Interface Policy...............................130
Appendix I- Vancouver Industrial Interface Policy............................ 132
Appendix J- Victoria Industrial Interface Policy............................... 134
Appendix K- Winnipeg Industrial Interface Policy 135
Appendix L- Communities of Calgary... 137
Appendix M- Municipal and Industrial Activities Where Hazardous
  Substances May Be Found...138
Appendix N- Abbreviations Used in Tables 3.1-3.4............................ 139
Appendix O- Interview Guide... 140
Appendix P- Interview Transcripts... 141
Appendix Q- Forest Lawn ARP Industrial Interface Policies................. 150
Appendix R- Inglewood ARP Industrial Interface Policies.................... 152
Appendix S- Manchester ARP Industrial Interface Policies....................154
Appendix T- Millican-Ogden ARP Industrial Interface Policies.............. 156
Appendix U- Millican-Ogden CRP Industrial Interface Policies.............. 158
Appendix V- Ramsay ARP Industrial Interface Policies........................160

References... 163

List of Figures and Tables

Figure 1.1- Calgary's Central Core 1900..8
Table 2.1- Visual Screening and Buffering Requirements..................... 30
Table 2.2- Minimum Acceptable Acoustic Levels.............................. 35
Table 2.3- Canadian Residential-Industrial Interface Policy Matrix......... 41
Figure 3.1- The Industrial Areas of Calgary...................................... 57
Figure 3.2- Northwest Quadrant Residential-Industrial Interfaces............58
Figure 3.3- Northeast Quadrant Residential-Industrial Interfaces............. 58
Figure 3.4- Southwest Quadrant Residential-Industrial Interfaces............58
Figure 3.5- Southeast Quadrant Residential-Industrial Interfaces............. 58
Table 3.1- Residential-Industrial Interfaces in Northwest Calgary........... 61
Table 3.2- Residential-Industrial Interfaces in Northeast Calgary............. 61
Table 3.3- Residential-Industrial Interfaces in Southwest Calgary........... 62
Table 3.4- Residential-Industrial Interfaces in Southeast Calgary............. 62
Figure 3.6- Residential Land Use within 200 m of Industrial Land Use..... 63
Table 3.5- Nuisance Only Residential-Industrial Interfaces................... 66
Table 3.6- The Most Problematic Residential-Industrial Interfaces.......... 67
Figure 4.1- ARP Policy Review and Comments of Senior Planners......... 87
Figure 5.1- MIACC Guidelines for Acceptable Levels of Risk................ 95
Figure 5.2- Appropriateness of Interface Policy Options for Calgary........ 102

Chapter One
Industrial Land Use Planning in Canada and Calgary

> At 11:35 am on August 9, 1999, the first of several massive explosions ripped through the Hub Oil Recycling Plant in Northeast Calgary. The fire involved a myriad of assorted buildings with approximately 80 storage tanks and vessels on site, the majority containing highly flammable material, acids, and distillates. Two of the largest vessels, which were full at the time, contained 60 000 and 65 000 gallons of distillates each.
>
>
>
> The Hub Oil fire- Aug. 13, 1999.
> Courtesy: Calgary Fire Dept.
>
> Two individuals lost their lives in the initial explosion and fire. Five others escaped with some minor injuries. Complete evacuations were ordered for a two-block radius as multiple explosions continued to spread through the plant, sending a shower of debris and droplets of oil throughout the surrounding neighbourhood. Minutes later, the evacuation zone was extended to an eight-block radius. Police and fire crews evacuated over 2000 people from the surrounding neighbourhoods. Residents were not allowed back into the area until the following day.
>
> In fighting the blaze, fire crews made a conscious decision to protect the perimeter rather than risk further lives with the ongoing and significant explosions. With the continued threat of explosions, the Hub Oil Refinery fire was one of the most dangerous in Calgary's history.
>
> Following the fire, the immediate communities affected and the residents involved were put through a traumatic and difficult time throughout the entire event and aftermath clean-up. (from background information prepared by the City of Calgary Disaster Services Committee for the Report on the Status of Disaster Preparedness in the City of Calgary. Dec. 8, 1999).

1.1 Introduction

The Hub Oil fire was one of worst industrial disasters in Calgary's history. Industrial incidents occur on a daily basis in Calgary, and around the world. Not all incidents are of the terrifying scale of the Hub Oil fire. However, one of the worst industrial accidents that has occurred in recent times was the 1984 incident in Bhopal, India that saw the release of toxic material from a fertilizer plant resulting in the evacuation of 200 000 people and 3000 fatalities.[1] The Bhopal incident dwarfs the Hub Oil fire both in terms of environmental damage and loss of life. It was the Bhopal event and the location of significantly dangerous industrial sites in Canada close to populated areas that lead to the initiation of much of the recent research into industrial location guidelines that will be referred to later in this paper.

Chapter One- Industrial Land Use Planning in Canada and Calgary

Most industrial incidents are of a significantly small scale and limited to the industrial site. However, when an event occurs and causes off-site injury or negatively impacts adjacent land uses, the event becomes known to the public and becomes an issue larger than a matter of internal plant management. When industrial enterprises are located next to populated areas, concerns are raised about the appropriateness of residential and industrial land uses situated next to one another.

Large industrial incidents can attract the attention of policy makers and the public-at-large to the plight of adjacent residents. However, there are less dramatic and cataclysmic activities occurring at industrial and residential land use area interfaces that go unnoticed by the public but may strongly affect each area. For an assortment of reasons, industrial areas are located next to residential areas in cities. In Calgary, for example, Hub Oil was located next to a residential area, separated only by a road, because the business occupied a land use district in which it was legally entitled to operate. Moreover, Hub Oil had been in operation since 1935, and the adjacent neighbourhood was not built out until 1958. Except for the explosion, and subsequent destruction of the plant, the area would still be inundated by the problem activities occurring at the interface. Currently, the site sits vacant, awaiting redevelopment once the contamination crews have finished the clean up. It is critical to remember that industry has a right to locate in a designated area in which the use is permitted. Residential district neighbours oftentimes know well before developing adjacent land or moving into the adjacent area exactly what uses are occurring in the industrial area. Policy makers should anticipate the interface conditions and these foreseeable issues should be addressed before people settle next to an industrial area.

Sensationalized events such as fire and explosions at industrial sites attract the attention of media, senior politicians and the citizenry-at-large. More mundane complaints about traffic and noise generated by an industrial neighbour are much more difficult to classify, measure, and address, especially when existing land use policy permits land uses that may produce such nuisances. Oftentimes it is difficult for industrial and residential land uses to act as comfortable neighbours. This is the situation in which a land use policy intervention can better the quality of the interface and reduce, or possibly eliminate, the problem.

The purpose of this paper is to **create land use policy recommendations that will significantly reduce the problems that occur where industrial and residential land use districts meet.** It is impossible for land use policy to keep another Hub Oil incident from occurring; industrial incidents will occur no matter how safe industrial operations can become. Effective policy, however, can minimize the impact of industrial activity on adjacent land use districts.

In order to begin the process of developing policy recommendations for improving residential-industrial interfaces, this paper will begin with an examination of the history of land use planning. This first section will continue with an overview of the history of industrial land use planning in Canada, and, more specifically, Calgary. The opening chapter will conclude with a description of citywide policy dealing with residential-industrial interfaces, including the Calgary Land Use Bylaw and the Calgary Plan.

Chapter Two will include a comprehensive review and comparison of residential-industrial interface policy employed by other municipalities across Canada.

Chapter Three will delve into the specifics of the problematic interface. The issues and conditions arising at interfaces will be defined and explored. The industrial areas of Calgary will be listed and all of the problematic interface areas will be identified. The different types of residential industrial interfaces in Calgary will be sorted into a classification typology.

Chapter Four will summarize Calgary community scale plans, in the form of Area Redevelopment Plans (ARPs), that concern some areas identified in Chapter Three as the most problematic interfaces. Interviews of City of Calgary planners will be conducted to further critique the success of ARPs.

Chapter Five will present the policy recommendations synthesized through the creation of this report. The recommendations will bring together the concepts described in the opening four chapters of the paper to address possible methods for resolving issues at problematic interfaces in Calgary.

1.2 The Origins of Land Use Planning

City planning is defined by the Merriam-Websters Dictionary as "the drawing up of an organized arrangement (as of streets, parks, and business and residential areas) of a city."[2] This definition provides a simplified description of this multifaceted process. Van Der Ryn and Cowan claim that "in reaction to the rapid, haphazard growth of cities in the industrial era, city-planning practice as it developed in the early twentieth century zoned development into separate single-use land areas for housing, industry, commerce, and recreation."[3] Organizers of cities throughout history have been faced with the "perennial issue called the allocation of land use or, what some may call, what goes where. These uses include the places for people to live, to do business, to govern, to worship, and the means for people and goods to circulate among the various land uses."[4]

Whether through legally binding statute or cultural understanding, there has always been a differentiation of land, and the purpose, if not the use, of that land. Certain areas are described as home, which is the site of family growth and daily life. Other areas not viewed as home are differentiated because they are either not in the same place as home or are the focal point of different activity. "Over time, mankind figuratively and literally began to plant roots into the land and from that evolved the notion of exclusive dominion and control over that land into which one put his labour."[5] Land Use Planning is the division of these spaces into legally binding districts. Before the advent of land use planning tools, districts hosting different uses existed in all human communities. Although home, work, and other uses did intermingle in the same building and land uses did intertwine in a more organic mix of uses, there have always existed places where certain uses were accepted and others were not. The structured religious or military activity of most cultures was likely to occur at a specific site at a certain time, and many other uses were prohibited from the site. Cities of early Greece, Mesopotamia, China, and the Fertile Crescent all separated land in this fashion. In many ancient cities, the market was separated from the residential areas, and the sacred religious sites were separated from everything else, and given the predominant location in the settlement.

Some form of land use separation has accompanied human civilization, regardless of whether or not official statutes have been in place. In many settlements, some form of statute has been in place in the guise of building laws or codes. "Long before zoning, there were regulations dealing with [development] factors in order to assure public health, structural safety, and fire prevention."[6] Not until the onset of the industrial revolution did the separation of land uses become codified as land use planning.

Before modern planning was invented at the turn of the twentieth century, the planning profession was not a profession at all, and the role of what would be considered the modern day planner would have been carried out by architects, designers, and urbanists. The European tendency is still to refer to planners as urbanists; a term that connotes a multidisciplinary approach to urban issues unlike the more specialized title of city planner. It is arguable that the development of industrial uses in the city lead to the rise of modern day planning, with land use planning based on zoning or development control devised to separate incompatible uses from one another. At the onset of the industrial revolution, the health and safety hazards that developed from placing industry next to residential areas lead to the adoption of early ordinances that limited the placement of certain uses next to one another and the scale of such operations.

1.3 Europe; The Crucible of Organized Land Use Planning

It is possible to view the development of land use planning as one of the outcomes of the industrial revolution. As the industrial revolution began in England at the turn of the nineteenth century and quickly spread to continental Europe, and, most notably Germany, it had wide reaching effects on cities and people.

> The first effects of industrialization on cities at the beginning of the nineteenth century, including the development of modern science and engineering and the change and growth of cities at a rapid pace and unprecedented scale, were very largely positive. The results were tremendous increases in wealth, reflected in large numbers of new houses for the middle and upper classes. The pollution, overcrowding and other negative effects of industry were to come to the cities later, after the development of railway networks in the 1830s. The first factories were located near sources of water power. As the cities of the time were almost always built near navigable waterways, and the presence of waterfalls is not helpful to navigation, industry almost always began well away from existing cities.[7]

The industrial revolution marked a dramatic change in the methods of production. Technological innovation and the growth of urban markets signalled the end of the country artisan and the rise of the industrial businessman. Goods could now be produced at unheard of rates by machines that could do the work of many men, but people were still needed to operate the machines in the factories that produced the goods. These people left the rural hinterland and entered the cities in droves in the early half of the nineteenth century. This massive urban migration needed housing. Hodge provides the following comments about the Canadian situation, which resembled the European situation at the onset of the railway age, "housing for poorer segments of the population was left to the land adjacent to industry and railways; the large, generally linear area occupied by freight yards and industries was also difficult to cross without expensive underpasses or bridges."[8] Hodge continues, "in inland cities, when development did succeed in leapfrogging the railway it often resulted in the establishment of lower income residential districts on the, so to speak, wrong side of the tracks."[9] The new poor urban working class was housed in marginal areas of the city generally unfit for human occupation. The familiar scenes depicted in Charles Dickens' visions of early industrial London were repeated across the industrial centres of Europe.

Industrial growth proliferated at a mostly unchecked rate in Europe throughout the nineteenth century. As Laux describes, "haphazard factory development was epidemic, smoke, fumes, and particulate matter shrouded the atmosphere, uncontrollable fires were rampant and roadway systems could not cope with the volumes of traffic."[10] The industrial city became a chaotic cesspool characterized by filth and unconstrained health hazards. "It was the advent of intense industrial uses and vast areas of often squalid housing for factory workers that alerted nineteenth century communities to the fact that growth could present dramatic transformations."[11] The Germans town planners were the first to identify the effects of industry on city form. As Logan states, "German planners in the latter half of the nineteenth century observed that distinctive land uses and activities seem to perform their respective functions more effectively when congregated in distinct areas. The planners could then organize the growth of industrial cities to ensure efficiency for the factories and amenability for the workers' housing."[12] Placing houses next to industry was convenient for industrialists and workers because there was no need to build the expensive infrastructure to transport the worker to his job. This proximity of worker to job site posed immense health risks for workers and often resulted in the construction of low quality housing stock and degraded environmental conditions.

New conceptualizations of the organization of cities appeared in Europe at the turn of the twentieth century. The German approach to land use planning was to, as Hodge puts it, "differentiate the regulations according to the needs of uses located in their respective districts. The practice became known as districting in Europe, and later, zoning, especially in North America",[13] as will be described in section 1.4. Planners were separating uses based on the impact of one land use on an adjacent land use. The scale of nineteenth century industrial operations often worked to destroy urban systems that had developed over thousands of years. "Government action discouraged and often ruthlessly eliminated the older, more organic concept of mixed uses in close proximity. Architects focused on creating new prototypes for single-use buildings. These templates inevitably neglected edges and interfaces with other systems."[14] This ignorance of interfaces as part of larger systems continues today in the form of transition zones that do not adequately recognize the need to provide a gradient of land use intensity between industry and other land uses. The resultant interface areas with a long history of incompatibility of uses are oftentimes the most difficult to reconcile.

The rise of land use planning and the understanding that certain land uses should be separated is apparent in the planning theories espoused in the late nineteenth century. In 1898, Ebenezer Howard unleashed the Garden City concept on a world that did not come to appreciate the work until years later. One of the main tenants of Howard's work is that industry should be separated from workers by a green belt. This was now possible because streetcar and rail service had become a common mode of mass transit in large cities around the world. A common view of the time was that a major problem of city life was the deterioration of living conditions. This fuelled the popularity of the Garden City concept, "which aimed to disperse the population and industry of a large city into smaller concentrations, and further, create community living environments in a new setting more amenable than those of the city. A main tenant was the arrangement of land use to promote convenience and reduce conflict."[15] Tony Garnier, in 1899, furthered the concept of residential and industrial separation in his Cite Industrielle. The civic centre of the Cite Industrielle was flanked on both sides by residential neighbourhoods, these areas were separated from the railway yards, port, and industrial districts by a park, and the whole city was surrounded by parklands. Europe was coming to terms with its industrial past and devising innovative methods with which to solve the problems of the hundred-year old industrial city.

1.4 Industrial Land Use Planning in North America

An examination of Canadian, and to a lesser extent American, industrial land use planning begins in the latter part of the nineteenth century. "Municipalities in all countries experiencing industrialization in this period, including Canada, sought to regulate the siting of buildings and the provision of basic services for safety and health reasons."[16] The regulation of state land in Canada, and specifically Alberta, "has been mainly a matter of local responsibility and concern."[17] The BNA Act of 1867 divides powers between the federal and provincial levels of government in Canada. Municipal Institutions in the Province are listed as one of the Exclusive Powers of Provincial Legislatures.[18] In turn, each province established legislation governing the management of municipalities." In Canada, municipalities continue as the primary managers of land use, with each province individually organizing the way in which municipalities are to be structured.

As in Europe, North American cities in the late 1800s were employing ordinances as methods of controlling building construction. Height restriction rules had been established in California in 1886, Washington, D.C. in 1889 and Boston in 1909.[19] Significant industrial enterprises had existed in the eastern United States and Canada since the early part of the nineteenth century. The problems of many European cities, including the health and fire hazards produced by factories in close proximity to residences, existed in the larger manufacturing centres of North America. "Attempts had been made to simply separate residential from non-residential uses within cities, the earliest Canadian bylaw being enacted in 1903, in London, Ontario."[20] Shortly thereafter, the Toronto bylaw of 1904 attempted to control "the location, erection, and use of buildings for laundries, butcher shops, stores, and manufactories."[21] Regulations were in place but they were not capable of controlling land use on a citywide scale. This lead to the development of zoning as a land use control tool.

Building regulations alone were incapable of controlling problems associated with the growth of unregulated industrialization and "the terrible living conditions of the poor in slum districts that occupied large urban areas."[22] Municipalities had the power to enforce safety,

---

" In Alberta, the Municipal Government Act (MGA) outlines the general jurisdictional responsibilities of municipalities. The MGA (2002) states that "a council may pass bylaws for municipal purposes respecting the following matters: the safety, health and welfare of people and the protection of people and property; nuisances, including unsightly property"; and others.

health, and structural standard on an individual property basis,[23] but not until the first comprehensive zoning ordinance was passed in New York in 1916 were cities capable of controlling land use on a district by district basis. The time had come for North American cities to adopt zoning regulations en masse. "Minimizing the potential nuisances and noxious side effects of industrial operations formed a major part of the rational for zoning."[24] As Hodge points out in the case of Toronto, "the various health, safety, and occupancy regulations were usually enacted on a district-by-district basis. Some areas were not regulated at all or only partially, and these often turned out to be where poor people lived as tenants. Planners began to urge comprehensive zoning bylaws that would provide not only greater uniformity of application of regulations but also a city-wide view on private development consistent with the view of the community plan."[25] The 1915 Ottawa-Hull plan is representative of the plans adopted by cities just before the rush to adopt land use bylaws in the 1920s. The plan outlines that "the authorities take steps to segregate industry into certain areas, to control the districts devoted to business and light industry, [and] to control and protect the residential districts."[26]

Kitchener was the first Canadian municipality to adopt a comprehensive zoning bylaw in 1924. By the end of the 1920s, most other large Canadian municipalities had followed suit and adopted their own zoning bylaws. Zoning, as described by Hodge, is the "planning instrument that deals with the land uses and the physical form of development on individual parcels of privately owned land. It deals, essentially, with: (1) the use that may be made of a parcel of land, (2) the coverage of the parcel by structures, and (3) the height of buildings."[27] Soon after these zoning ordinances were adopted in North America, court challenges arose, testing the claim that zoning must universally apply to all properties within respective zones. In the United States, where individual property rights are entrenched in the constitution, many court challenges sought to strike down zoning as too restrictive. "In Canada, neither the BNA Act nor the Charter of Rights entrenches property rights. Thus, there is not the same legal basis in Canada for zoning or reason to limit land-use regulation to that form of bylaw."[28] Therefore, Canadian industrial land use planning has ventured from the strictly zone based model of the American system. Many municipalities in Canada, based on the rules set out by their province, use some form of development control which, "allows for each development proposal to be reviewed to ensure consistency with the aims of the emerging plan and a development permit issued as warranted."[29]

Since the advent of zoning in the 1920s, Canadian municipalities, with Calgary as no exception, have gravitated toward a system of land use that incorporates parts of the American zoning system and development control. This hybrid system allows for permitted uses in certain zones, but retains certain development control at the discretion of the municipality. This hybrid system has wide reaching implications for industrial land use planning in Canada, and, more specifically Calgary, which will be explored later in this paper. The inflexibility of the zoning system and difficulties with managing the discretionary power of development control can result in the presence of problematic industrial residential interfaces. "Physical forms in a community have a remarkable persistence even though the original function of the place may change. The planner, in any period, therefore works with the legacy of the past decisions about a community's physical form."[30]

1.5 The Early Industrial History of Calgary

The City of Calgary owes its existence to the North West Mounted Police fort built at the confluence of the Bow and Elbow Rivers in 1875. Fort Calgary soon attracted local aboriginals and trappers, hunters, and profiteers to settle in the area. The fledgling community surrounding Fort Calgary struggled to survive as little more than a trading outpost and military installation until the arrival of the Canadian Pacific Railroad (CPR) in 1883 at the eastern bank of the Elbow River. As rumours abounded about the impending arrival of the CPR earlier in 1883, people descended upon the town from the surrounding region and Europe. At the time European and eastern North American cities were developing ways to rectify the squalor of their industrial slums, Calgary was becoming an established settlement, with town incorporation occurring in 1884. The coming of the railway was the direct impetus for industrial growth to commence. In other railway towns across the country, industrial firms were encouraged to locate near the freight terminals or along rail lines. Calgary was no exception, as, "in 1888, Calgary council established a policy giving generous tax exemptions, free building sites, and bonuses to individuals manufacturing virtually any product."[31] Soon after the railway arrived, East Calgary, the area of the town located on the east bank of the Elbow River, emerged as the manufacturing area. This area continues to function as an industrial area to this day.

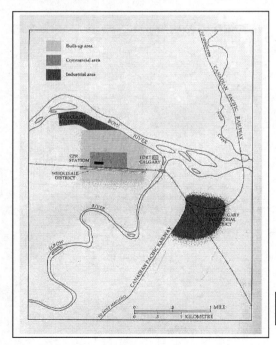

"Railroad development, while undoubtedly a boon to the economic development of communities, strongly affected the pattern of their growth. Typically, the railway passenger station anchored one side of the downtown commercial area, and on the other were the freight yards and industrial area. Housing development spread out from this core, but not evenly, for the freight yards proved to be both a physical and psychological barrier to residential growth."[32] This situation held true for Calgary. The rail line and physical barriers of the rivers and escarpments to the north and southwest limited the growth potential of the city. As figure 1.1 shows, the industrial sector of early Calgary was located close to the rail line.

Figure 1.1- Calgary's Central Core 1900 (Foran, 1978)

In 1886, town authorities persuaded the CPR to build stockyards on section 11 just outside the town limits where "the prevailing wind would not carry the offensive effluvia from the yards over the town."[33] The problems associated with placing residential districts next to industrial areas have been around since the early days of Calgary, and are not necessarily limited to adjacent neighbourhoods. Industrial development continued unabated in East Calgary. In fact, "in the 1880s, east Calgary landholders, fearful of the western movement of the business centre, encouraged industries to locate on their properties outside the corporate limits."[34] The stockyards and brewery located in East Calgary and the Eau Claire lumber mill and smaller enterprises located between the river and the downtown business centre ensured these areas would be dominated by manufacturing activity for years to come.

By 1905, Calgary was established as an important regional distribution centre as the city was served by the east-west CPR line, the north-south Calgary-Edmonton line, and the short-lived Grand Trunk Pacific railway (the company ceased operations but the track remained). "The small manufacturing base established in the 1880s expanded to meet regional demands, and according to the 1911 census, Calgary counted 46 establishments employing 2133 workers."[35] "A strong economic base was needed to ensure economic stability within the city. Inglewood [in East Calgary] with all of its main railway lines, nearness to water and low land areas, was a natural location for industrial expansion."[36] With the 1913 recession looming, Calgary was selected as the site of the Ogden CPR repair shops in 1912. The shops were built as a locomotive repair facility and were located in Ogden, 8 kilometres from the townsite. A residential community sprung up around the site, and problematic land use issues continue to this day at the interface of the residential community and heavy industrial repair shops.

Up until 1911, "manufacturing land use followed precedents set in the 1880s with locations near railways in the east and southeast of the city. Residential areas were encouraged within manufacturing districts."[37] This all changed in 1911, as Foran explains,

> The city's greatest success in directing land-use patterns resulted from the industrial policy of 1911, which outlined procedures that were followed with reasonable consistency. The overall result of the municipal policy was the consolidation of manufacturing enterprises in suitable locations with adequate provision for future expansion. Since its building bylaw did not provide for purely industrial districts, the city included inducements in its industrial policy, but these were limited by provincial statute. The city was to purchase suitable industrial areas, and industries were then attracted to these districts through the extension of uniform concessions. Since the city was able to provide utility and transportation services, the municipally owned areas were more attractive than privately owned properties. The industrial policy of 1911 gradually moved manufacturing concerns from high-rent locations to sites in designated industrial areas.[38]

To this day, the City of Calgary outranks private developers as the largest developer of industrial land in the city. The 1911 policy was followed up by the creation of the building bylaw of 1912, which provided fairly lenient regulations for construction and lot size (most lots were built to a 25' frontage). A later bylaw was enacted in 1914 that was designed to limit building height to 6 stories. This regulation functioned as a fire prevention measure as water pressure within City hydrants was insufficient to reach higher levels. Also in this year, the British planner Thomas Mawson and other planners "were convinced of the need to design residential subdivisions which would form a whole with the industrial areas they served."[39] Even though the streetcar network began in 1909 and grew rapidly to reach areas as far-flung as Ogden and Bowness, it was still deemed important to locate residences next to industry. Provisions were included to plan for the two distinct land uses as a whole system. The city followed a policy of encouraging "the erection of workmen's houses near the industrial areas. Sometimes the city's purchase of property for industrial sites was contingent upon subsequent land being made available for residential purposes."[40]

The development of Ogden and Manchester, located south of downtown between the railroad and MacLeod Trail, "helped establish a pattern of residential enclaves in areas which became increasingly industrial."[41] A small remnant of this development still exists in Manchester, and will be highlighted in greater detail in Chapter Four. Industrial development continued throughout the Calgary region, and, in 1924, the Royalite Company drilled a well at Turner Valley that opened up a vast reserve of wet gas that ignited flames in the air and was known to Calgarians for years as Hell's Half Acre."[42] The fire at the well site could be seen on the outskirts of Calgary, almost 50 km away, until the blaze was contained. According to Cormier, "major industries, under the guise of progress, had little respect for the human communities or natural environment they destroyed in their means to an end."[43] The planning decisions of 80 years ago still resonate in the attempt to remedy these long standing incompatible land use issues.

The Alberta Town Planning Act of 1912 "instructed municipalities to take steps to provide orderly and planned growth."[44] In 1913, further legislation was enacted prohibiting municipalities from granting bonuses or providing tax exemptions to industrial establishments."[45] In 1929, "the Alberta Town Planning Act empowered cities to appoint town-planning commissions whose mandate would include the preparation of a zoning bylaw. Although the new bylaw, adopted in 1934, allowed for four districts instead of two [residential and business] and provided for single family, two family, and multiple dwelling districts, it only applied to the inner city area."[46] Zoning had arrived in Calgary but at a limited capacity.

Industrial land use planning continued nearly without change until 1948 as the city's industrial policy of 1911 had provided ample land for expansion. "Most incoming industries were located in Manchester or in the adjoining manufacturing sites along MacLeod Trail. The city had also set aside acreage in the Nose Creek area for future industrial parks. Refining facilities were built in east Calgary, consolidating the manufacturing character of the southeast corridor between the stockyards and the Ogden repair shops."[47] By 1948, the very nature of industry changed in Calgary with the discovery of oil at Leduc, and Alberta's subsequent growth as an oil-producing province. "By 1965, virtually no aspect of internal economic growth remained unaffected by developments in the oil industry. Expansions in educational services, construction, retailing and manufacturing all reflected the dynamic growth of oil and gas enterprises."[48] Industrial districts were needed to serve the oil and gas industry, and the industrial areas east of the Bow River and around the airport were established and expanded rapidly. Also by 1965, development control was gaining credibility as it was elsewhere in the country, instead of the inflexible zoning principles which were perceived as prohibitive to effective planning.[49]

The industrial growing pains experienced in Calgary are endemic of the western Canadian experience. Calgary is a new city, but the problems associated with locating industry next to residential districts have not eluded Calgary. In fact, issues of incompatibility continue to arise at many of the older residential-industrial interface areas. Some of these areas have been in existence since before the turn of the century, and these areas will be highlighted in Chapter Three. The disaster at the former Hub Oil site and subsequent escape of hazardous materials into the adjacent residential areas, as introduced at the beginning of this chapter, illustrates what can happen when land use incompatibility issues are not addressed.

1.6 Industrial Land Use Districts

Zoning and other land use planning tools have increased in complexity over time. The original Calgary zoning bylaw included two different zones. The zoning bylaw was, soon after, expanded to include four zones. This growth in the number of different zones has continued to this day. At the present time, there are 35 different land use districts used in Calgary. The land use regulation tool, known by a variety of names, has been revisited 8 times, with another bylaw review currently underway (See Appendix A for a list of these bylaws). Calgary hesitates to use the word zone because of the hybrid system of zoning and development control employed in the City. Instead, the City employs the term Land Use District.

The vast majority of municipalities across North America employ a land use districting system that divides land use into different classifications. This creates residential, commercial, and industrial districts that are somehow differentiated from one another. Within each district is included a list of uses that are allowed to locate within the district and the various rules and regulations governing the district. As mentioned in the previous sections, Calgary includes both discretionary and permitted uses within each land use district. Permitted uses "are the uses for which an applicant is entitled to a permit as of right if the proposed development conforms with all the applicable provisions of the land use bylaw. Such uses ought to be approved as a matter of course no matter where they are located in the district, provided that the development standards set out in the bylaw are also met."[50] Discretionary uses allow for greater development control, but the planning process can become long and involved. "The listed discretionary uses, while generally appropriate for the district, are those that are of such a nature that they may or may not be reasonably compatible with neighbouring uses, depending on the circumstances."[51] Zoning allows for certainty in the minds of developers and a degree of expediency in developing a project in a reasonable amount of time.

Industrial districts also adhere to this model of subdivision within each industrial district. Municipalities typically will divide industrial uses into districts based on the intensity and scale of the industrial tenants. Industrial activities of a large scale and of a significant processing component "whose external effects are likely to be felt beyond the boundaries of the site and perhaps beyond the boundary of the district itself"[52] are usually described as heavy. Smaller manufacturing, fabricating, processing, production and storage operations tend to be located in a light industrial district. Other industrial districts may include office type industrial parks and industrial areas with a commercial element. Haar points out the diverse nature of industry, "some [industries] need vast docks for unloading ore or sugars from overseas while others are quite content with a good connection with the highway for light trucks; some store mountains of coal, raw materials, or waste upon their land, yet many need little in the way of bulk; and still others must get rid of great volumes of industrial waste whose improper disposal has polluted so many of our rivers."[53] The separation of industrial land use into subcategories will be addressed in the upcoming section for the City of Calgary, and in the following chapter for a sample of other municipalities in Canada. There is not one particular division of land uses that will work for every urban situation. There are industrial land uses found in a port city like Vancouver that would be completely inappropriate for a landlocked industrial area like those found in Calgary. However, strategies concerning how industries are to be located in certain districts may be more appropriate than the methods espoused by land use regulations currently in place. Districting according to permitted and discretionary uses, as is the current popular approach to land use planning, is not the only method for deciding what industries can go where.

The division of industrial land use districts can be accomplished in a variety of ways. Many municipalities use the traditional system of dividing land use according to the land uses that are excluded from operating in the district. Other municipalities provide exhaustive lists of the uses that are permitted or discretionary within each district. Lighter industrial areas tend to exclude heavy industry and other larger industrial operations. Also, older land use bylaws in Calgary allowed for all of the uses allowed in lower intensity districts to be permitted in heavier industrial areas. This is no longer the case, as different districts have become more specialized and developed individual land use regulations. Some municipalities, through bylaw review processes, are now developing new ways of looking at the industrial sections of their land use or zoning bylaw. Division of industrial districts based on land use alone is seen as antiquated in some cities. Some municipalities are adopting performance-based approaches to industrial land use planning, which will be highlighted in the next chapter.

The division of industrial districts has important implications for residential-industrial interfaces. Certain municipalities place a greater emphasis on the relationship of industry with adjacent land uses within policy documents. As will be shown in the next section, the interface between industry and residential areas is not a critical component of the industrial sections of the Calgary land-use bylaw. Heavy industrial areas tend to have a potential for greater negative impacts on residential neighbours. However, this does not always hold true, as certain types of uses in light industrial areas can produce significant problems for neighbours. Although, "there are numerous plants that anyone would be glad to claim as neighbours, whose lawns are green, whose walls gleam, where quiet reigns,"[54] there are industrial neighbours that will never be an appropriate neighbour of residential areas. Conversely, higher density residential neighbours can disrupt the ability of industrial neighbours to conduct their business through parking and traffic intrusions into the industrial area.

1.7 Calgary Policy Concerning Residential-Industrial Interfaces

The current Calgary Land Use Bylaw (LUB) was approved on March 3, 1980. The Calgary Plan was approved as the City of Calgary Municipal Development Plan in 1998. The residential-industrial interface policies written in the LUB and the Calgary Plan will be analyzed in this section.

1.7.1 The Calgary Plan

According to the Plan itself, "the Calgary Plan is the pre-eminent plan guiding growth and development within the City of Calgary."[55] The plan acts as the municipal development plan for the city as required by the Alberta Municipal Government Act. As the overall vision of growth for the City to the year 2024, the plan provides broad policies for the overall growth and management of all aspects of life in the City. Included within these policies is a plan for the industrial future of Calgary, including mention of the residential-industrial interfaces. Relevant policies from the plan are outlined below.

- **Assist the community in improving environmental quality** (Policy 2-1E).[56]

The context of this policy is broad in scope; environment is meant to encompass all commonly considered types of environments; water quality, air quality, natural areas, and land. Areas of incompatible land use can be described as low in environmental quality with the potential for pollution to affect the environmental quality of the neighbouring community.

- **Industrial Growth Strategy** (Policy 2-2.2.6).[57]

This policy deals specifically with Calgary industry. "Where residential uses have developed in close proximity to existing industrial uses, it is important to explore options for mitigating or eliminating any problems or conflicts that may have developed. The continued viability of existing businesses should be a prime consideration in the resolution of problems."[58] The interests of residents shall not compromise non-problematic industrial areas.

- **Encourage the relocation, where appropriate, of low intensity, functionally obsolete or incompatible non-residential land uses in the built-up area to peripheral areas and encourage vacated sites to be developed for more appropriate uses** (Policy 2-2.2.6E).[59]

This policy outlines that obsolete incompatible land uses should be moved in order to place compatible land uses next to one another. This policy may counter policy 2-2.2.6, which reinforces the importance of considering the business in the resolution of problems. This policy provides the impetus for utilizing creative means with which to redevelop underused or vacated industrial lands.

- **Protect appropriately located industrial development from undue encroachment of residential development in cases where the nature of the industrial activity requires separation from residential uses** (Policy 2-2.2.6G).[60]

This policy is intended to encourage industrial areas to remain apart from new residential developments, and, just as importantly, allow them to remain economically viable. Industrial areas that may produce significant adverse affects are important to the economic vitality of the City and the Plan recognizes the need to protect industry in certain areas from residential uses that may hamper industrial operational capacity.

Summary   The Calgary Plan recognizes that incompatible land uses should be separate. According to Calgary Plan policy, any assessment of conflicting land use areas must be completed on a site by site basis to improve the quality of the affected community and protect the viability of the business interest.

Conclusions   The range of issues covered within the Calgary Plan is enormous. The plan supports the notion that residential and industrial land uses should be separate from one another, however, there is no vision for the types of intriguing and viable places current residential-industrial interfaces could become. Because of the scope of the Calgary Plan, it cannot provide a future vision for such a specific type of interface in a city containing a myriad of planning related issues. The problematic residential-industrial interface areas can be dealt with through consultation with communities and industry in a much more detailed process. Traditionally, this has occurred in the Area Redevelopment Plan (ARP) creation process. ARPs are created for specific geographic areas to address an assortment of issues in the area. The success of several Calgary ARPs in remedying particular problems at residential-industrial interfaces will be assessed in Chapter Four. The potential exists to address interfaces using other types of policy, including issue specific policy that can be applied to the city as a whole instead of being replicated for individual areas.

1.7.2   The Calgary Land Use Bylaw

The LUB is organized into sections concerned with different land uses in the City. Section 43 deals directly with industrial district land use rules. Calgary has organized its industrial land use districts separating uses based on the intensity of industrial use. There are four industrial districts in Calgary, ranging from lower impact office-style business parks creating few, if any, noxious by-products to limited service large scale industrial enterprises.

The City of Calgary also uses a Direct Control (DC) District designation that "provides for developments that, due to their unique characteristics, innovative ideas or because of unusual site constraints, require specific regulations unavailable in other land use districts. This district is not intended to be used in substitution of any other land use district in the LUB that could be used to achieve the same result."[61] This being written, the DC district has been used to create land use districts closely resembling the land use districts described in the bylaw.[≅] However, the vast majority of residential-industrial interfaces occur between residential and industrial districts, and not DC districts. Where an interface exists between a residential or industrial DC district, it will be noted in tables 3.1-3.4 found in Chapter Three.

[≅] In some cases the change between the DC district and district after which it is modelled can be the exclusion of one particular land use. This situation has occurred in all land use districts, including industry. Instead of being used to create truly innovative land use districts, the DC districts are used to slightly alter the regulations of the bylaw. The result has been a promulgation of the use of the DC district so that approximately 1700 different DC districts now exist in Calgary, the vast majority of which are very similar to existing land use districts. This rampant use of DC districts creates a confusing situation for people attempting to solve issues at areas of land use disputes because the rules governing DCs are frozen at the date the DC was adopted. It becomes difficult to administer the exact rules in place for any specific DC because of the numerous LUB amendments that have been adopted since 1980.

The industrial policies in the LUB relevant to residential-industrial interface areas are outlined below. The policies below are identified by the numbering systems used in the LUB.

- **General Rules for Industrial Districts in Calgary- Industrial Performance Standards** (Section 43.1). "The purpose of the performance standards in the control of industrial uses is to permit potential nuisances to be identified; to ensure that all uses will provide methods to protect the community from hazards and nuisances which can be prevented by processes of control and nuisance elimination; and to protect industries from arbitrary exclusion based solely on the nuisance production by any particular type of use in the past."[62]

The LUB calls for the separation of industry from incompatible land uses, but attempts to protect the interests of businesses at the same time. The LUB identifies that minimum performance standards are needed, but does not prescribe specific standards within the bylaw. Air contaminants, visible, and particulate emissions, odorous matter, and toxic matter are not to exceed levels proscribed by the Clean Air Act of the Province of Alberta. Fire and Explosive Hazards are under the jurisdiction of the Fire Prevention Bylaw. Finally, there is mention that "all on-site lighting shall be located, oriented, and shielded so as not to adversely affect the adjacent residential properties."[63] As will appear throughout this summary, the LUB addresses the need to remedy a potential problem but does not prescribe specifically how it is to be done.

- **General Rules for Industrial Districts in Calgary- Landscaping** (Section 43.8). "Where a landscaped area is required, it shall be provided in accordance with a landscape plan and in conformity with the landscape requirements and standards."[64]

The bylaw prescribes that "all plant materials shall be of a species capable of healthy growth in Calgary and shall conform to the standards of the Canadian Nursery Trades Association for nursery stock."[65] The bylaw also contains regulations for minimum sizes of deciduous and coniferous trees and shrubs to be planted. The minimum ratio for tree planting is "one tree per 45 square metres of landscaped area provided."[66] The bylaw stops short of naming specific species appropriate for planting in industrial properties.

- **I-1 Industrial-Business Park District** (Section 44). "The purpose of this district is to provide for comprehensively-designed business parks comprised of uses which can be conducted entirely within buildings and structures."[67]

This is the least common industrial district used in Calgary, so uncommon that there are no I-1 districts in Calgary. I-1 industrial parks would contain the least noxious producing industrial uses. The business tenants would carry out business operations within the building and would, ideally, produce few of the problems traditionally associated with industry, including noise, odour, and other emissions. The I-1 district would, if used, contain the high-tech and communication industries found in suburban office industrial parks across North America. The I-1 district section contains the following policies pertaining specifically to residential industrial interfaces:

- **Performance Standards** (Section 44.3.a). "No use or operation shall cause or create any conditions which may be objectionable or dangerous beyond the building which contains it, such as the following: noise, odour, earthborne vibrations, heat, or high brightness light sources."[68]

Definitions of each condition created by industrial operations will be supplied in Chapter Three. It is interesting to note that there are only five conditions identified in this section of the bylaw. Chapter Three will show that there are many more conditions that need to be considered and entrenched in the LUB. These performance standards do not indicate what levels of conditions produced by industry are acceptable or what thresholds should be maintained.

- **Interface Treatment** (44.5.a). "Where a site abuts a residential district, the treatment of the interface in terms of distance, visual screening and landscaping shall be to the satisfaction of the Approving Authority."[69]

The approving authority is to employ the landscaping requirements and standards appearing in section 43.8. The approving authority (the Development Officer or agency working in the interest of the City) has been unable to curtail the presence of problematic residential-industrial interfaces even though they have discretionary power over the quality of the interface. This might be due to insufficient attention paid to specific development applications, a lack of knowledge of the potential problems caused by a particular use, administrative oversight caused by overwork in the development department (a strong possibility in the hectic Calgary context), or insufficient bylaw enforcement conducted by the City. This policy is insufficient in assuring that both industry and adjacent land uses achieve an acceptable level of compatibility.

- **I-2 General Light Industrial District** (Section 45). "The purpose of this district is to provide for a wide range of general light industrial and associated uses which are compatible with each other and do not adversely affect surrounding non-industrial land use."[70]

The performance standards are the same as for the I-1 district, except the range of objectionable conditions is extended from the building to the boundary line of the site. The interface treatment is different from that for I-1, as expressed in policy 45, "where a site abuts, or is separated by an intervening street from, a residential district, an expressway, a major street, the treatment of the interface in terms of distance, visual screening and landscaping shall be to the satisfaction of the Approving Authority."[71] The industrial site need not border the residential neighbour directly for the City to treat the interface. The I-2 district is the only industrial district in which permitted uses become discretionary uses:

- "on sites that abut, or only are separated by an intervening public thoroughfare from a residential district, a freeway, an expressway or a major street, and
- "in existing buildings on sites that abut, or are only separated by an intervening public thoroughfare from a residential district or a PE (Public Park, school, and recreation) district."[72]

This regulation, if properly employed, gives the Approving Authority the ability to control the industrial uses locating next to residential areas even if they would normally be considered a permitted uses in an I-2 district not abutting a residential area. If used consistently, this regulation could effectively manage the placement of industrial operations ensuring only low impact externality producers located next to residences.

- **I-3 Heavy Industrial Districts** (Section 46). "The purpose of this district is to provide for manufacturing, assembling and fabricating activities, including large scale or specialized operations whose external effects are likely to be felt to some degree by surrounding districts. In addition, those uses with established functions in the economy but having a well known nuisance potential are to be permitted only within this district."[73]

It is recognized the effects of some I-3 activity will reach into neighbouring districts. These districts will ideally be lighter industrial or other non-residential areas. The I-3 district includes the large-scale industrial enterprises synonymous with the manufacturing, assembly, and processing that takes place in mass production and refinery operations. This section does not include a policy for performance standards, although the purpose of the section outlines that external effects of these operations are likely to be experienced in adjacent areas. The uses within this district may produce adverse affects so intense that the only way to soften the impact of the activity is to provide an undeveloped buffer zone around the industry. Heavy industry may produce "emissions of noise, odour, smoke, and particulate matter, along with heavy traffic volumes, not to mention their generally unappealing appearance."[74] Heavy industries serve an important function in municipalities as they "are a vital source of property taxes and a key generator of employment and demand for goods and services."[75] Municipalities must balance the need for safety of the citizenry from potentially harmful industry with the desire to allow economically important industry to continue operations.

- **I-4 Limited-Serviced Industrial District** (Section 47). This district is intended to "provide for those uses requiring large tracts of land with minimal or no land servicing requirements."[76]

The now familiar performance standards and interface treatments are the same as those written for the I-2 district. These districts are located in rural environments at the City's outskirts not yet fully connected to City services.

Summary Each of the four industrial district sections within the Calgary LUB recognize, in the interface treatment policy, the importance of applying visual screening and landscaping to the interface to the satisfaction of the Approving Authority. The landscaping requirements, outlined in Section 43.8 of the bylaw, deal primarily with the planting of trees around the industrial area to act as a visual screen. Performance standards are also mentioned within three of the land use district sections, however, the conditions of industrial operations listed in the bylaw are limited to noise, odour, earthbourne vibrations, heat, and high brightness light sources. The description of industrial performance standards is expanded in the General Rules for Industrial Districts Section (43), but the bylaw refers issues associated with air contaminants, visible and particulate emissions, odorous matter, and toxic matter to the measures prescribed in the Clean Air Act of Alberta. The conditions covered in the provincial legislation are to be enforced by the province. Likewise, fire and explosive hazards are to comply with the Fire Prevention Bylaw and are enforced by the Fire Department. Other industry produced negative externalities are not listed in the bylaw, but may appear in other legislation.

Conclusions The bylaw does recognize that industrial district uses are to be compatible with each other and shall not adversely affect surrounding non-industrial land uses. However, the nature of the interface between the land uses is to be determined to the satisfaction of the Approving Authority. The bylaw is insufficient in controlling the possible formation of problematic residential-industrial interfaces because:

- The list of industry produced negative externalities is incomplete.

- Details concerning the regulation of performance standards are incomplete. It is insufficient to merely refer the control of industrial conditions to provincial regulations or other Calgary regulations. It must be made explicit what level of government is responsible for monitoring specific performance standards. There must be "clear recognition that Alberta municipalities are empowered through the Municipal Government Act to police low level, non-health or environmental related nuisance level violation."[77]

- There are permitted uses within each district that may be inappropriate neighbours for residential areas and might be considered for deletion from particular land use districts. For example, the permitted use, "Manufacturing, fabricating, processing, assembly, disassembly, production or packaging of material, goods or products,"[78] appears too vague and inclusive to adequately separate incompatible uses.

1.8 Conclusion

A Hub Oil style disaster occurs infrequently but the possibility exists that a smaller-scale event can occur. Land use policy in Calgary can be created to ensure that the effects of both large-scale disasters and smaller scale nuisances are minimized at the interface of industrial and residential districts. The development of land use planning tools originated in an attempt to improve the appalling urban conditions that prevailed in European and North American cities as a result of the changes to the scale of industry and the organization of the new industrial city. Zoning and development control was invented to ensure that certain types of land uses were separated from one another. It has become common practice to separate home from industry, but there has been inadequate treatment concerning what to do where these separated land uses meet. Calgary's industrial history begins at the time of the arrival of the railroad, and industrial areas still exist where the first CPR line crossed the Elbow River. The urban form of Calgary has evolved to include areas where industrial districts and residential areas meet. Calgary planning policy has attempted to improve the quality of these interfaces but the problems for both industry and residential areas at these interfaces persist. Current citywide policy, in the form of the Calgary Plan and Land Use Bylaw fall short of providing sufficient detail for remedying Calgary's various interface issues. Chapter Two will focus on what other large Canadian municipalities have done to remedy their problematic residential-industrial interfaces. The lessons learned and policies employed by other cities will provide a clearer understanding as to how Calgary can better address its own problematic interfaces.

Notes

[1] MIACC, 1997.
[2] Merriam-Webster, 2002.
[3] Van Der Ryn and Cowan, 1996.
[4] Hodge, 1991.
[5] Laux, 2002.
[6] Hodge, 1991.
[7] Barnett, 1986.
[8] Hodge, 1991.
[9] Hodge, 1991.
[10] Laux, 2002.
[11] Hodge, 1991.
[12] Logan, 1976.
[13] Hodge, 1991.
[14] Van Der Ryn and Cowan, 1996.
[15] Hodge, 1991.
[16] Hodge, 1991.
[17] Laux, 2002.
[18] Great Britain, 1867.
[19] Haar, 1957.
[20] Hodge, 1991.
[21] Toronto, 1904.
[22] Barnett, 1986.
[23] Hodge, 1991.
[24] Schwab, 1993.
[25] Hodge, 1991.
[26] Ottawa-Hull, 1915.
[27] Hodge, 1991.
[28] Levin, 1957.
[29] Hodge, 1991.
[30] Hodge, 1991.
[31] Foran, 1978.
[32] Hodge, 1991.
[33] Calgary Tribune, 1886.
[34] Foran, 1975.
[35] Foran, 1978.
[36] Cormier, 1975.
[37] Foran, 1978.
[38] Foran, 1978.
[39] Calgary, 1914.
[40] Foran, 1978.
[41] Foran, 1978.
[42] Gray, 1975.
[43] Cormier, 1975.
[44] Foran, 1978.
[45] Foran, 1978.
[46] Foran, 1978.
[47] Foran, 1978.
[48] Foran, 1975.
[49] Foran, 1978.
[50] Laux, 2002.
[51] Laux, 2002.
[52] Laux, 2002.
[53] Haar, 1957.

[54] Haar, 1957.
[55] Calgary, 1998.
[56] Calgary, 1998.
[57] Calgary, 1998.
[58] Calgary, 1998.
[59] Calgary, 1998.
[60] Calgary, 1998.
[61] Calgary, 1980.
[62] Calgary, 1980.
[63] Calgary, 1980.
[64] Calgary, 1980.
[65] Calgary, 1980.
[66] Calgary, 1980.
[67] Calgary, 1980.
[68] Calgary, 1980.
[69] Calgary, 1980.
[70] Calgary, 1980.
[71] Calgary, 1980.
[72] Calgary, 1980.
[73] Calgary, 1980.
[74] Laux, 2002.
[75] Laux, 2002.
[76] Calgary, 1980.
[77] Farr, 2002.
[78] Calgary, 1980.

Chapter 2
Interface Land Use Policy in Canadian Municipalities

2.1 Introduction

As illustrated in Chapter One, the Calgary Land Use Bylaw is a statutory regulation that defines the types of development appropriate for the four different industrial land use districts. The LUB and Calgary Plan act as the umbrella documents that are intended to shape the policy later created at the community scale. Individual communities have used the ARP adoption process to develop policies that are intended to remedy the problems associated with residential-industrial interfaces. These ARPs will be discussed in Chapter Four. The focus of this chapter remains at the broader citywide scale.

This chapter will highlight the residential-industrial interface land use policies of other municipalities across Canada. Where possible, the land use policy document and Municipal Plan of each of the listed municipalities was scrutinized to determine how each municipality deals with its residential-industrial interface issues. Because they operate within the same national political and social climate, and share common histories of urban development, only Canadian cities were selected. Although many examples from the United States and other countries exist, it is the intention of this report to document which strategies have been employed in the Canadian setting. Municipality comparison and analysis was based upon the following criteria:

- A major city with a population similar to Calgary
- A significant industrial land use component and legacy of industrial use in the city
- Availability of current residential-industrial interface policy

Although it is difficult to describe exactly what makes a city major, this report will define a major city as a significant regional business and cultural centre with a population over 200 000 people. In most instances, cities were selected with a population nearer the Calgary level of 900 000 people. Secondly, only cities with a major industrial component or long history of industrial activity were selected. In the Canadian experience, larger centres tend to include historic and current industrial development. Most major centres of today have been prominent industrial areas for many years and in part owe their existence to an industrial heritage, be it derived from the railway, mining, processing, manufacturing or other activities.

There was a degree of difficulty in locating significant policy concerning residential-industrial interfaces for some cities. In some instances, in the cases of Montreal and Quebec, the problem was one of language. In other instances, mention of the residential-industrial interface was not included in the policy. In the third instance, current municipal mergers in cities in Ontario and British Columbia meant the most recent policy would be obsolete as new mega-municipalities developed new citywide development guidelines. However, the municipalities included herein provided many examples of diverse and unique interface treatment options.

2.2   Canadian Municipal Industrial Interface Policy

The citywide policies pertaining to the residential-industrial interfaces of each municipality are summarized in this section. Within each summary are comments describing how the policy attempts to manage the land use of interface areas and how the policies may operate in the Calgary urban context. More detailed descriptions of each policy are located in the Appendices. A table comparing the relevant interface policies of each municipality can be located in the last section of this chapter. The municipalities selected for comparison with Calgary in this report are:

Edmonton	Toronto
Hamilton	Vancouver
Ottawa	Victoria
Regina	Winnipeg
Saskatoon	

2.2.1   Edmonton

Both the cities of Calgary and Edmonton function under the auspices of the Municipal Government Act of the Province of Alberta. Edmonton and Calgary are roughly the same population and the cities owe much of the their economic prosperity to the abundance of oil and gas in Alberta. However, the predominance of older and more prominent industrial areas in Edmonton leads to the presence of more industrial pockets in Edmonton and a greater attention to the issue in the city. This is reflected in the creation of the Industrial Business district in the City zoning regulations. Following are policy highlights of Plan Edmonton and the Zoning Bylaw. Sections dealing directly with the residential-industrial interface have been summarized. The more generalized municipal plan will be described first, followed by the more specific zoning bylaw. Specific policies of the plan and bylaw can be found in Appendix B.

2.2.1.1   *Plan Edmonton: Edmonton's Municipal Development Plan*

Like the Calgary Plan, Plan Edmonton acts as the pre-eminent planning document for the entire City of Edmonton. Edmonton also uses community scale ARPs, but this examination will focus on citywide policy.

Summary   Plan Edmonton is similar to the Calgary Plan in that it provides wide reaching statements for managing residential-industrial interfaces. However, the idea of risk management is introduced in Plan Edmonton. The incorporation of Risk Management into Plan Edmonton stems from the location of several large-scale industrial operations in close proximity to residential districts in the Edmonton area. These operations tend to be the oil-related industries located on the eastern edge of Edmonton. As the potential for a large-scale industrial accident exists, the plan has identified the need for including emergency preparedness and risk management into municipal land use policies.

Conclusions   Edmonton industrial land use management has shifted towards the idea of risk management and preparedness. Preparing sufficiently for risk at industrial site interfaces will preclude certain incompatible uses from locating there. Risk management will serve a land use function; the measurement of potential risk at a significant level will keep certain uses from locating within certain distances from a potentially hazardous site. This notion of Risk management pioneered by the Major Industrial Accidents Council of Canada (MIACC) is described in greater detail in Chapter Five. Plan Edmonton also calls for older industrial areas within the city to be preserved while mitigating problematic interfaces; Edmonton has done this by creating a residential-industrial interface transition land use zone to buffer the two land uses. This zone will be highlighted in the following section.

2.2.1.2   Edmonton Zoning Bylaw 2001

- **(I)Industrial Business Zone**

The City of Edmonton employs a performance standards and risk based approach to industrial land use zoning. All industrial uses are allowed uses in the (I) Industrial zone, but the potential development impacts are assessed to help decide whether or not each development applicant is suitable to the site. This approach gives the development approving authority of the City control in deciding which uses can locate where according to the forecasted levels of on-site and off-site impacts. Also, the land use on-site can be monitored and controlled as the nature of the operation evolves, creating the opportunity to enforce industry compliance with the specific regulations specified in the Industrial Statutory Plan, which would function as an area specific plan overlay (much like an ARP). Industrial uses can be monitored to ensure compliance with the original Statutory Plan, instead of attempting to ensure businesses remain compliant with generalized industrial land use districts like those employed in Calgary. However, the approving authority has greater responsibility in monitoring that each performance standard is measured within the Statutory Plan for each individual industrial land use. Because of the amount of industrial land use in Edmonton, it may be difficult to coordinate particular departments to measure performance standards and maintain staffing for periodic monitoring. However, the idea of managing land use based on projected on and off site impacts, instead of which particular uses are appropriate, may be applicable to the Calgary situation.

As an example, in the Edmonton Industrial Business (IB) zone, general industrial uses are permitted, but the scale of operation is subject to the on-site and off-site measurement of impacts. A small-scale toy maker may be an appropriate neighbour for a residential area, but a larger toy factory is completely inappropriate. The potential off-site implications of a larger manufacturer can be measured in order to keep the business from locating in a potentially problematic zone. Traditional zoning might allow manufacturing in a light industrial district, allowing both of the above businesses to locate, without recognition of how the scale of the business, and the consequential impacts, will affect the neighbouring areas.

The Edmonton noise bylaw is similar to that of other municipalities (information concerning the Calgary Noise Bylaw is highlighted in Appendix C). It is important to note that the Edmonton Zoning Bylaw recognizes the noise levels that must be met by operations located next to Residential Zones. In fact, "where two districts with differing noise levels abut each other, the noise level standard to be met shall be that of the district with the lower permitted noise level."[1] The Calgary LUB does mention specific levels of noise compliance and refers to the Calgary Noise Bylaw.

The Edmonton Zoning Bylaw continues, "no use or operation shall cause or permit to be caused, any conditions that may be objectionable or dangerous beyond the boundary line of the Site that contains it, such as the following: odorous and toxic matter, dust, fly ash or other particulate matter, vibrations, air pollution, industrial waste, water quality deterioration, groundwater quality or quantity deterioration, glare, radiation emissions, or high brightness light sources."[2] The bylaw continues that compliance is expected with other federal, provincial, or municipal enactments. The Zoning Bylaw lists the specific conditions that may be objectionable beyond the boundary line of the site. Edmonton includes a list of ten potentially adverse conditions, which, along with others, will be defined in Chapter Three. Including detailed performance standard regulations concerning conditions within the jurisdiction of the municipal level of government would not only clarify the acceptable levels of adverse conditions for affected adjacent residents, but for industrial developers and city staff as well.

The Development Regulations for Sensitive or Special Areas states two critical points. Firstly, the bylaw states that "no operation or activity shall emit air or water contaminants in excess of the standards prescribed by the province of Alberta, pursuant to the Environmental Protection and Enhancement Act or by the City, pursuant to the Sewer Use Bylaw."[3] Like the Calgary LUB, the Edmonton Zoning Bylaw must comply with the Provincial Environmental Protection and Enhancement Act (called the Clean Air Act in the Calgary LUB). Secondly, the Edmonton Zoning Bylaw sets out that "an assessment of Risk may be required for any proposed development that, based on the MIACC List 2 of Hazardous Substances[=], may be expected to generate a level of risk through fire, explosion, major release or other hazardous event that could have an adverse impact beyond the site of the facility."[4] The idea of risk assessment is incorporated directly into the bylaw and the assessment would be carried out to the satisfaction of the Emergency Response Department (ERD). This risk assessment would ensure the activity conducted and materials stored at the site did not produce an inappropriate level of potential risk.

Four other industrial zones exist in Edmonton. The zones are:

- **(IB) Industrial Business Zone**
The City reverts to the standard permitted and discretionary use model of land use in this section of the bylaw. General Industrial Uses remains as a permitted use in this section of the bylaw. The size and scale of the general industrial use is not controlled by the risk assessment and performance standards system used in the (I) Industrial zone. To further control the size and scale of the industrial operations in this zone, Edmonton may have been better served placing certain types of industrial use into the discretionary use section. For example, manufacturing is permitted in this zone as it is one of the uses described as an Industrial Use in section 7.5.

There are fewer permitted uses in this zone than in the Calgary light industrial district. An equivalent to the IB district is not found in Calgary and a new district could be created in Calgary to better control the industrial uses at problematic residential-industrial interfaces. However, Edmonton may be having difficulty controlling noise and odour conditions produced

---

[=] The MIACC List 2 of Hazardous Substances was developed by members of MIACC with expertise in the areas of toxicology, health and safety, emergency response and enforcement. The list was compiled through the examination of already existing lists of hazardous substances and the lists are drawn up to reflect the Canadian experience. No updated list exists as MIACC was disbanded in 1999.

by certain business in the IB zone because manufacturing, one of the uses that produces negative externalities, is permitted in this transitional zone.

The Zoning Bylaw makes no mention of the possibility of any kind of hybrid live-work accommodation existing within this land use district. There appear to be areas in Edmonton, around the Whyte Avenue area, where the provision of studio live-work space for artists and cottage industrialists might be successful.

- **(IM) Medium Industrial Zone**

- **(IH) Heavy Industrial Zone**
    The uses found in this zone are to be the greatest producers of possibly harmful negative conditions. General Industrial Uses that create "nuisances that extend beyond the boundary of the site or have a deleterious effect on other zones due to their appearance, noise, and odour"[5] are expected to locate in this zone. These zones would form the core of industrial areas and would tend to have the most distance separating the business uses from incompatible uses.

- **(IS) Special Industrial Zone**
    This zone resembles the I-1, Industrial Business Park district of Calgary's LUB.

Summary The performance based standards approach to industrial planning attempts to organize the placement of land uses according to their on and off site impacts, and not according to zoning by type of use. For the (I) Industrial Zone, businesses are not guaranteed certainty of land use in the district just because they are a permitted use; the development applicant must ensure that potential conditions of production will meet certain performance standards in regards to the noise, odour, and other conditions created.

Conclusions Ideally, industrial areas would exist with IH zones at the centre, and less obtrusive industrial zones radiating out from this core. Around the IH zone would be found an IM district, bordered by IS and IB districts at appropriate interfaces. This model also exists in Calgary, however the I-1 district is not used and no Industrial Business district exists. The continued popularity of the catchall I-2 district creates the possibility for problematic interfaces to propagate. The potential exists to rethink how interface districts are designated in Calgary. The industrial zoning rules in Edmonton are different from the Calgary land use designation rules in two critical ways:

1. the Edmonton Zoning Bylaw introduces the idea of risk management and performance standards in deciding where specific uses may locate. The possibility of the production of potentially harmful or negative conditions is addressed before the development is built.

2. Edmonton provides a buffer land use zone to shield incompatible industrial uses from other incompatible uses (and vice versa), protecting the viability of the industrial area and the abutting area, which is typically residential.

2.2.2 Hamilton

The City of Hamilton is currently undergoing a municipal merger with several outlying municipal entities being incorporated into the new megacity. As such, the new city is undergoing planning policy updates at an unprecedented scale. The Hamilton land use planning document was written in the same year as the Calgary LUB, and the new city plan is being produced at the time of this summary, and therefore could not be included in this report.

2.2.2.1 Hamilton Zoning Bylaw 1980

The Hamilton Bylaw provides sparse mention of residential-industrial interfaces. The bylaw is limited to prescribing lot coverage limits concerning industrial uses located adjacent to residential districts. The policies can be located in Appendix D.

Summary and Conclusions The bylaw serves as an example of how some regulations only briefly mention the issue of industrial-residential interfaces. An interesting follow-up to this brief summary would be to view how the new zoning bylaw and plan for Hamilton have been altered in order to better address the interfaces as Hamilton has a long history of heavy manufacturing activity and port related activity.

2.2.3 Ottawa

Like Hamilton, Ottawa is currently undergoing a municipal consolidation. The Ottawa land use bylaw is currently under review and could not be included in this report. The following review of the city and regional plans is valuable in recognizing how the residential-industrial interface and associated issues are addressed at two different broad scales. The specific polices are located in Appendix E.

2.2.3.1 Ottawa Regional Plan 1999

The Ottawa-Carlton Regional Plan of 1999 does not specifically address the residential-industrial interface and issues occurring therein. However, related concerns are addressed in section 11, Development Constraints. The Plan is primarily concerned with the management of previously contaminated sites. The Plan states that former industrial sites must be defined according to their potential for contamination. This will greatly impact the potential for site redevelopment. The Plan spells out exactly what the development applicant must do in order to have the development reviewed.

If the potential for contamination exists, the Plan outlines the steps that must be followed in the Site Assessment process, including a Historical Land Use Survey. This type of survey will not stop a potential new interface from being developed, however, through the course of the survey, the presence of contaminants can be linked to past uses, thereby recognizing which former site uses may have created negative off-site conditions. If it is deemed that certain past uses were problematic for adjacent uses, than similar uses applying to develop the land can be halted, nullifying the chance of creating another problematic situation.

Industry is listed as a noise producer that policy is enacted to control, however the specifics of the noise regulations are not dealt with in this plan, but are addressed within the noise bylaw.

Summary and Conclusions The Ottawa Regional Plan was written before the merger of Ottawa area municipalities. There is no mention of specific interface areas and only noise and previous contamination are mentioned as potential interface conditions. Individual municipal plans would have to be consulted to determine interface treatment options. However, since the area is undergoing a retooling of the land use policy with the municipal merger, the only plan to be reviewed will be that of the City of Ottawa.

2.2.3.2 City of Ottawa Official Plan 1994

The Ottawa City Plan addresses the needs of the traditional industrial areas in the city. Often, in the examination of residential-industrial interface areas, industry is perceived as the villain. This is not always the case, as will be explored in Chapter Three. Although some industrial uses are best located far from residential areas, some smaller scale industrial areas are needed within the inner city to serve local consumers and other business. This situation is addressed in the Traditional Industrial Areas policy.

This Traditional Industrial Area is designed to protect industrial areas that might be irrevocably changed if allowed to evolve according to market conditions alone. In some inner city areas in Calgary, older mixed industrial areas are being converted into commercial or office areas. The close proximity of some of the traditional industrial areas to downtown make them prospective locations for office and retail developments that desire locating closer to the city core. However integral to the local business and residential community they might be, the industrial uses located in these central areas may be forced out of the inner city by market forces that dictate a higher price for land. Commercial and office uses that can afford the high cost of land locate where industry once located. The industry is pushed to the cheaper industrial areas at the city's periphery. A situation arises where all businesses and residents must travel to the city's periphery to access light industrial uses that may have once been a short commute away. There is a need for small print shops, bottle depots, and repair shops within the inner city. However, these uses are found where many of the problematic interfaces are located.

Summary and Conclusions Like Calgary, Ottawa recognizes the importance of viable industrial areas in the older areas of the city. Where residential-industrial interface issues are minimal, the industrial uses are to be encouraged to remain in the delineated Traditional Industrial Area. Creating these areas gives these districts a special designation apart from regular industrial areas. Calgary may consider creating special industrial areas in established areas to help preserve these essential areas and keep them from converting to commercial or other land uses. The Greenview industrial area is one such industrial area that serves an important local role in the city but is facing substantial redevelopment pressure to convert to different land uses.[6]

2.2.4 Regina

The 1999 City of Regina Zoning Bylaw provides the most specific rules encountered for landscape and buffer regulations. The pertinent parts of these regulations are described below, after a brief description of the Development Plan. The specific polices of the Zoning Bylaw can be found in Appendix F.

2.2.4.1 Regina Development Plan

The Development Plan recognizes the potential for problematic residential-industrial interfaces to occur. "Generally, it notes this situation is to be avoided."[7] Where a problematic interface does exist, the residential area shall be separated from the industrial use by a buffer strip. The buffer is defined as "a parcel of land provided as a separation space between industrial/residential lots, acting as a sound or visual barrier through the usage of vegetative materials, fencing screening and/or berming."[8] The specifics of the buffers are outlined in section 2.2.4.2.

2.2.4.2 Regina Zoning Bylaw 1992

The Regina Zoning Bylaw divides industrial uses into the standard subcategories of intensity of use, including the light, medium, and heavy divisions already described in the Calgary context. Some of the specific uses are different, but each zone is divided into the typical permitted and discretionary use categories.

- **Zone IIT: The Innismore Industrial Transitional Zone**
This zone includes a performance standards section outlining certain standards that are to be met, including yard and setback requirements, provision for tree planting and preservation measures, the location of illuminated signs, architectural control of new buildings, the storage of outdoor materials, and "anticipated noise levels, possible odours and the provision of a reasonable degree of privacy."[9] As has been shown in the Calgary example, there are no quantitative limits set for these standards (except for noise) codified in the Zoning Bylaw, and the Development Officer defines the standard limits in most cases. The success of these performance standards is not decided by an aggregate limit of compliance, but by the degree of rigor of the particular Development Officer.

- **The Noise and Obnoxious Use Regulations**
These sections are common to most industrial land use bylaws. The type of noise (constant or intermittent) is not adequately defined in the bylaw, even though a chart outlining noise level limits is included. Other performance standard measurement thresholds are not identified in the bylaw, and reference should at least be made to other regulations (possibly at a provincial level) in order for the bylaws to be interpreted consistently by planners and others using the Zoning Bylaw.

The key distinction of the Regina Zoning Bylaw is the inclusion of a section dealing with landscape and buffer regulations for the entire city. Different types of land use interfaces are described, and the residential-industrial interface is only one such area for which interventions are designed. The landscape and buffer regulations are not specifically laid out in the industrial sections of the Zoning Bylaw. Instead, landscape and buffer regulations exist in their own section and address a number of areas where these regulations are required.

- **The Landscape and Buffer Regulations**

This section acknowledges the need to provide a screen or buffer between incompatible land uses, like other city policy covered in this chapter. However, the Regina Zoning Bylaw includes tables of information suggesting specific types of vegetation that are appropriate to certain sites. This section includes lists of trees that are tolerant to certain conditions and appropriate for certain microclimatic areas. Including this list in the bylaw allows the planner and developer an opportunity to gauge which types of trees and shrubs may be appropriate to a prospective development.

- **The Visual Screening and Buffering Regulations**

This section of the bylaw does not function as a performance standard approach. Prescriptions for measuring the potential nuisances listed above are not described in the bylaw. Reference must be made to other bylaws and regulations concerning these nuisances. However, the requirement of a specific visual screen and buffer is determined according to the degree of incompatibility between proposed land uses. Table 2.1 shows the visual screen and buffer requirements between land uses based on the incompatibility of a proposed development and an existing land use. The regulations "shall apply to all new developments and substantial additions to existing developments in all land use zones."[10]

The table will inform whether or not a visual screen or buffer is required. The following procedure is then followed to determine what type of "visual screening or buffering is required:

- Step 1: Identify the type of proposed land use
- Step 2: Identify the land use abutting the proposed development site
- Step 3: Determine the visual screening or buffering required by referring to table 2.1
- Step 4: Select one or more of the allowable buffering or screening materials specified previously in section 15."[11]

The Regina Zoning Bylaw describes the visual screen or buffer that shall be provided as "a 1.8 metre high fence or masonry wall, a 1.8 metre high berm, soft landscape described previously in section 15, or a combination of the fence, berm, or landscaping."[12] The bylaw also dictates that the property owner shall be responsible for the upkeep of all buffers and screens.

Summary Regina has removed the issue of interface quality from different sections of the Zoning Bylaw and placed all landscape and buffer regulations within one section of the bylaw. The regulations governing many different land use interface conditions, and not only residential-industrial interfaces, are lumped together to provide specific regulations as to how these interfaces shall be managed. The size of berms and fences are specifically spelled out according to the type of land use located on either side of the interface.

Conclusions Regina provides an excellent example as to how regulations governing buffering requirements can be more specifically laid out to ensure compliance. The specific nature of the

Chapter Two- Interface Land Use Policy in Canadian Municipalities

regulations, right down to the types of trees and shrubs, ensures developers and planning officers should not be confused as to how the interface should be managed. Regina has organized existing and proposed land use classes in table 2.1 in a way specific to the Regina situation. A similar matrix could be prepared for Calgary that illustrates, in a graphic manner, whether or not a berm or landscaping is required. If an interface intervention is required, then the specific requirements of that interface could be included in the Zoning Bylaw or regulations located in another bylaw could be referenced.

Table 2.1   Regina Visual Screening and Buffering Requirements

		EXISTING ABUTTING LAND USE					
		Class 1 All 1 and 2 Unit Dwellings in Residential Zones and Non-Residential Zones*	**Class 2** All Uses in Residential Zones, except Class 1 Uses	**Class 3** All Commercial Uses, except Class 4 Uses	**Class 4** Selected Uses in Industrial and Commercial Zones**	**Class 5** All other Uses in Industrial Zones, except Class 4 Uses	**Class 6** All Land Uses in Special Zones
Proposed Land Use	**Class 1** All 1 and 2 Unit Dwellings in Residential Zones and Non-Residential Zones*	☐	☐	☐	☐	☐	☐
	Class 2 All Uses in Residential Zones, except Class 1 Uses	◆	☐	☐	☐	☐	☐
	Class 3 All Commercial Uses, except Class 4 Uses	◆	◆	☐	☐	☐	●
	Class 4 Selected Uses in Industrial and Commercial Zones**	◆	◆	☐	☐	☐	●
	Class 5 All other Uses in Industrial Zones, except Class 4 Uses	◆	◆	●	●	☐	◆
	Class 6 All Land Uses in Special Zones	◆	◆	☐	☐	☐	☐

KEY:
- ● Buffering required.
- ◆ Visual screening required.
- ☐ Buffering not required but may be provided.
- * Includes Detached Dwelling, Duplex, Semi-detached Dwelling.
- ** Includes Child Care Centre, Eating and Drinking Places, Entertainment, Hotel, Motel, Offices, Parking Areas, Personal Service Establishment, Recreation-Outdoor, Retail, Service Station, Shopping Centre.

(Source: Regina Zoning Bylaw)

2.2.5 Saskatoon

The interface planning policies for Saskatoon resemble those of Regina, as both cities are found in the province of Saskatchewan. Like Regina, Saskatoon employs a Development Plan that outlines a skeletal framework for development and a more specific Zoning Bylaw that divides the city into zones based on levels of intensity of use. Included at the conclusion of this section is a summary of a special discussion paper written in 2002 that pertains to residential-industrial interfaces.

2.2.5.1 Saskatoon Development Plan 1998

The Development Plan divides industrial land into three different land use policy areas. The three zones are described below.

- **Business Park**
Business Parks are to be developed to a superior level of quality than other industrial districts. The business park uses are to create no nuisances for adjacent districts, therefore allowing them to be placed adjacent to residential districts.

- **Light Industrial**
Light industrial zones are intended to act as buffers between heavier industrial areas and other land uses. This model is either made explicit or inherent in most of the industrial land use division schemes employed across Canada. The effectiveness of these schemes is strongly dependent upon which uses are excluded from operating in each zone.

- **Heavy Industrial**

Summary and Conclusions The Saskatoon Development Plan divides industrial uses into the standard industrial land use zones. The lists of permitted and discretionary uses are not listed within this document and are located in the Zoning Bylaw; there is no mention as to what factors dictate which specific uses may locate in each zone. The policies within each zone make broad-based comments about the need for buffers between noxious uses and residential areas.

2.2.5.2 Saskatoon Zoning Bylaw No. 6772, 1987

The most recent version of the Saskatoon Zoning Bylaw procured for this report was adopted in 1987. The 2001 Industrial Land Inventory, however, identifies "seven zoning districts used to implement land use policy in Saskatoon."[13] The Zoning Bylaw is a standard example of dividing uses into zones base on the intensity of use. The bylaw lists permitted and discretionary uses much like the other bylaws covered in this report. "As Saskatoon's economy diversifies, there will be a need for City Council to provide more differentiation between various types of industrial land in Saskatoon, both for marketing and regulatory purposes."[14] There is an underlying theme of the importance of economic development written into the Industrial Land Inventory Report. The zoning districts are different from the more generalized land use policy areas outlined in the Saskatoon Development Plan. Descriptions of the seven zoning districts can be found in Appendix G.

Summary and Conclusions Apart from the emphasis on economic development (it is written within the description of each zone), the Saskatoon zones are divided based on intensity of use. There are two different light industrial zones, one of limited activity and one of a wide range of uses. The limited use zone might be appropriate to interface areas in Calgary. Also, the RA zone could act as a catalyst for economic and cultural growth in areas where industrial uses are more compatible with adjacent uses, but where economic stagnation has occurred.

2.2.5.3   Municipal Enterprise Zones in Saskatoon, 2002 Discussion Paper

"An enterprise zone is a specified geographic area, usually an inner city neighbourhood, where incentives are offered by local and/or provincial governments to create a better environment for property investment and change. Incentives are usually economic and are designed to help reduce the deterrents associated with developing in the core. The purpose of an Enterprise Zone is to help to create positive change in the core neighbourhoods."[15] Although not a direct remedy for a problematic residential-industrial interface, the enterprise zone could act as a catalyst that encourages investment to an area where many of the problems are aesthetic and social. Vacant or dilapidated industrial areas create problems of a social nature that can be just as damaging to local communities as noise and pollution. Conversely, depressed communities can create problems for adjacent industrial areas through the dilution of social problems into business areas in the form of vandalism, squatting, prostitution and violent activity. Enterprise zones can help to revitalize business areas, which in turn may improve the quality of the physical and social life of adjacent residents. Ignored residential interfaces could improve through this redevelopment. An objective of an Enterprise Zone is to "provide relocation assistance to help resolve historical land use conflicts."[16] If the land use conflict is beyond mending, the Enterprise Zone can aid in moving a business or land use without impairing its ability to continue functioning in a viable way.

One of the factors identified as a key indicator of neighbourhoods at risk, or in decline, is "land use conflicts. There are two opposing forces at work in some core neighbourhoods- there are long-time industrial tenants who want to grow their business in an economical location, and there are long-time residents who want the quality of their neighbourhood to improve. In some instances, due to historical circumstances, there are heavy industrial uses situated immediately adjacent to residential uses."[17] This is also true for Calgary. Residential-industrial interfaces are often located in lower rent areas. Improving the interface may be detrimental to both residents and industry, increasing rental costs for residents and business owners. However, many interface areas are of such low quality that the continued presence of incompatible land uses next to one another is unacceptable for both land use occupants.

Summary and Conclusions Economic incentives may act as a powerful tool to promote redevelopment of economically stagnant communities. Using these same incentives to relocate businesses from traditionally problematic land use conflict interfaces may also be effective, and this strategy could be included in citywide or community plan policy. These areas described as at-risk by the city of Saskatoon are often home to small businesses and residents who cannot afford to locate elsewhere. Economic incentive programmes designed to improve the area may prove successful, changing the nature of the area completely and removing a long-standing community. Before an economic incentive programme is initiated, it will be critical to envision what type of community is desired, whether it be populated by a reinvigorated community of long time residents or a new community of gentrified businesses and homes.

2.2.6 Toronto

The official plan for the new mega-city of Toronto was published at the time of writing this report and sections of the plan summary are reviewed below. The 1987 plan will be reviewed because of inclusion of the Mixed Industrial-Residential Area. The newest version of the Zoning Bylaw was also difficult to locate as Toronto is characterized by a myriad of planning documents pertaining to the former independent municipalities now comprising Toronto.

2.2.6.1 Toronto Official Plan Part 1, 1987

Similar to the Development Plans of the Saskatchewan cities summarized in this report, Toronto lists generalized land use areas within its official plan. The policies that deal with industrial areas with mention of adjacent uses are listed in Appendix H.

Toronto is comprised of many older and more varied industrial areas than more recently established western cities. Older industrial areas in Toronto have likely gone through changes in use before zoning and land use controls were implemented early in the 1920s. Industrial uses mix more readily in Toronto with other land uses in an organic fashion; the **Mixed Industrial-Residential Area** land use area identifies that these mixed use areas should contain a wide range of uses without impinging on the environmental well-being of adjacent uses.

Traffic is mentioned as a potential problem that should be addressed by council. Also, other bylaws are to be created to manage the production of negative externalities. The Council is also expected to ensure other factors are considered as they arise in a particular mixed-use area.

Summary and Conclusions The Mixed Industrial-Residential Area would likely be unnecessary in the Calgary context because of the lack of mature, fully integrated mixed-use areas in the city. However, there are smaller areas in Calgary characterized by a mix of older industrial buildings situated next to residential buildings. In these areas, there is little mix between the industry and residences. The Toronto example could be used in Calgary to create smaller, direct control integrated communities where light intensity industrial uses are compatible with residential uses within the same community.

2.2.6.2 Toronto Official Plan Summary, 2002

The new plan for Toronto calls for the division of the city into eight different land use designations. Four of the designations reinforce existing physical character and four are intended for growth. The two areas relevant to residential-industrial interfaces are listed in Appendix H.

- The **Neighbourhood** is intended to preserve residential uses and small-scale stores and shops in existing communities. The plan calls for the conversion of outmoded land uses in established neighbourhoods to increase housing opportunities.

- **Regeneration Areas**
These areas are designed for managing growth in the city by opening up former industrial and institutional areas to a variety of uses. Toronto has built upon the ideas contained in the Mixed Industrial-Residential section of the 1987 plan to create Regeneration Areas that can contain an even wider range of uses in the same block or building. These areas will be managed according to the policies developed in a Secondary Plan that will provide policy details at the scale of the affected area.

Summary and Conclusions The 1987 and 2002 Toronto Plans recognize the presence of mixed-use areas in the city as sites of continued redevelopment. The areas should remain as mixed-use areas where different uses can coexist. Instead of prohibiting uses from locating next to one another or to be separated, the 2002 plan calls for different uses to potentially intermingle in the same building. The success of this policy rests in the details created in the Secondary Plans as to how land use conflicts are to be remedied.

2.2.7 Vancouver

Vancouver employs a land use planning approach based on zoning, unlike the mixed zoning and development control system used in Calgary. Like other cities, Vancouver outlines the general goals of the city within the city plan. The creation of the general plan for Vancouver involved an intensive public participation process and the plan is a generalized vision for the future of Vancouver. The Zoning Bylaw is specific in its treatment of industrial zones and how they are to interact with adjacent incompatible land uses.

2.2.7.1 Vancouver CityPlan, 1995

The issue of problematic residential-industrial interfaces is not addressed specifically in the plan and the only relevant policy is listed in Appendix I. Like Calgary, Vancouver recognizes the need to protect industrial areas where they might otherwise be prone to conversion to another use. Also, Vancouver is a fully developed city unable to expand, and, unless amalgamation occurs with neighbouring municipalities, it will remain this way. There is no ability to build residential communities on greenfield sites in this city, which creates more pressure to place housing units on non-traditional sites. Current and former industrial areas may become popular sites for residential redevelopment because of this shortage of developable land on the periphery.

2.2.7.2 Vancouver Zoning and Development Bylaw No. 3575

Like other municipalities in British Columbia, Vancouver uses more zoning categories than Calgary. Whereas the hybrid land use system employed in Calgary allows for DC districts to be used more often (therefore eliminating the need to create more land use districts), BC cities have worked within the rigidity of the zoning system to create zones applicable to specific areas in the city. The industrial districts used are outlined below.

- **MC-1 and MC-2 Districts**

    The Vancouver Zoning Bylaw provides an explicit vision of the type of place to be created in this district. Where other cities balk at the inclusion of value-based statements in the land use bylaw, Vancouver includes, within the intent section of the district description, that building designs should "contribute to area character and pedestrian interest."[18] These goals are inherently difficult to measure; it is even more difficult for a developer, planner, community, politician and other interest group to come together on an consensual understanding of what defines area character.

    Dwelling units are a conditional use in this zone in conjunction with any of the permitted uses listed in the zone description. The Development Permit Board (DPB) considers the design and livability of the proposed dwelling unit before the residence is approved. In a multiple unit conversion project, the DPB considers the "quality and livability of the Multiple Conversion Dwelling, the suitability of the building for conversion in terms of age and size, and the effect of the conversion on adjacent properties and the character of the area."[19] Discretionary decision making is in the hands of the DPB, and it is their responsibility to ensure that developments in this district adhere to the intents of the district. This district also allows for the provision of a residential unit associated with, and forming an integral part of, an Artist Studio. Vancouver has a sizeable artistic community in pockets around the city and this district recognizes their needs for live-work space.

    The MC-1 and MC-2 districts also make provision for exposure to sunlight. Section 4.10.1 states that "all habitable rooms in buildings used for residential purposes shall have one window on an exterior wall."[20] This is intended to reduce the construction of suites in the interior of multi-use buildings and ensure some exposure to natural light.

    The district schedule includes a provision for the measurement of noise. Under section 4.15 Acoustics, it is written, "a development permit application for dwelling uses shall require a noise measurement."[21] Table 2.2 shows the acceptable noise levels in different parts of the dwelling unit.

Table 2.2   Minimum Acceptable Acoustic Levels for MC-1 & MC-2 Dwellings

Portions of Dwelling Unit	Noise Level (Decibels)
Bedrooms	35
Living, dining, recreation rooms	40
Kitchen, bathrooms, hallways	45

The inclusion of this small table reiterates the notion that although residential uses are allowed in this mixed-use district, they must still comply with certain performance standards. Residential uses will not be allowed in a mixed-use area with a high level of noise experienced in the residence. The kitchen area of the proposed residential use must not have a sound measurement over 45 decibels, which, according to the Calgary Noise Bylaw chart found in Appendix C, is the sound level found in an average urban home located next to a quiet street. This is a strict noise level restriction, and if enforced, will ensure residential uses are not placed in noisy areas, or are built of materials that will shield the residence form excessive noise. The inclusion of this quantitative performance standard directly within the bylaw is much more effective than simply mentioning that noise is a problem to be addressed; referring to a standardized level of performance clarifies problem areas for the users of the zoning bylaw.

- **M-1, M1-A, M-2, and I-2 Districts**

    M-1 districts are not intended to be located at the interface of residential areas. The M-1A district differs from the others in that all uses in the district are conditional.

- **M-1B District**

    This district is designed to protect industrial uses from certain commercial and office uses that may infiltrate an industrial area. The type and scale of non-industrial uses is restricted.

- **IC-1 and IC-2 District**

    Commercial uses are allowed in this mixed-use industrial area. Advanced technology industry is often perceived as an acceptable neighbour for residential neighbours and is encouraged to locate in this district. External design regulations are included "to achieve a form of development compatible with the function and character of abutting major streets. The specific intent is to achieve building continuity that contributes a unified image to development along major streets in the IC-2 District."[22] These design regulations are intended to minimize the effect of industrial developments on the consistency of the existing streetscape. The new developments are to recognize and emulate the existing pattern of the street front developments.

- **IC-3 District**

    This zone would create a lively arts and theatre district complete with a residential component and light industrial area likely made up of small-scale cottage industry shops. There are mature mixed-use areas in Calgary, including Inglewood and Ramsay, that may be appropriate for this type of district zoning.

- **I-1 District**

    This district would appear to function as the catchall district for most industrial areas and most closely resembles the Calgary I-2 district.

- **I-3 District**

    The high technology industry is expected to act as a suitable industrial neighbour for residential areas.

Summary Many of the districts described in the Vancouver Zoning and Development Bylaw are similar in intent to one another. Specific regulations may vary only slightly from those of other districts. However, the different districts are applied in specific areas and are attuned to the specific conditions of that area. There is mention of the interface with adjacent land uses within the description of each individual district. The importance of the relationship between industrial and residential areas is addressed in each zone of the industrial section of the bylaw.

Conclusions Vancouver has opted to use a land use system that is composed of several different land use district types. There are twelve different industrial districts, unlike the four found in the Calgary LUB of which only three are used. The use of more districts allows for some zones to better address the particular land use issues in an area. Some of the districts are quite specific and can, in a detailed manner, dictate the future land use pattern of the area. Calgary's use of a limited number of unique land use districts may hamper its ability to address the specific planning needs of specific areas. It may be argued that the division of industrial districts into too many different districts makes land use management confusing. However, the City of Calgary uses DC districts that are very similar to standard industrial land use districts that may only deviate from standard districts by the exclusion of one permitted use. Calgary, in effect, has created many more industrial land use districts than Vancouver, which are even more difficult to manage because of their status as DC districts. The use of a wider range of area specific industrial districts may better manage the range of issues occurring at residential-industrial interfaces.

The inclusion of table 2.2 into the body of the Vancouver Zoning and Development Bylaw clarifies the noise performance standard which is often left up to the discretion of the approving authority or Development Officer. Placing quantitative performance standard values in the bylaw simplifies which levels of compliance must be followed. Legal problems may arise if the noise bylaw is not referenced in the zoning bylaw, but ensuring that regulations are standardized should only be a matter of maintaining interdepartmental communication.

2.2.8 Victoria

Victoria is similar to Vancouver in that industrial districts are used to manage the land use of specific geographic areas. In fact, the Zoning Regulation Bylaw that predates the current bylaw included 17 different industrial districts. The Official Regional Plan and Victoria Zoning Bylaw are described below.

2.2.8.1 Victoria Official Regional Plan 1974

The Victoria Official Regional Plan of 1974 is the oldest plan included in the policy comparison section of this report. Although 28 years old, the plan mentions industrial areas specifically and the possible problems associated with incompatible land use interfaces. The official plan designates three types of industrial areas, including Established Industrial Areas, Potential Industrial Areas, and Industrial Conversion Areas.

- **Established Areas**
  These areas consist of areas already used by industrial businesses.

- **Potential Industrial Areas**
  These areas are future industrial land use areas.

- **Industrial Conversion Areas**
  These areas exist as industrial areas in waiting and the uses currently existing on site are to be removed when the site is deemed suitable for conversion back to industrial use. The plan

recognizes that industrial uses adjacent to "existing or proposed residential, commercial, park and agricultural areas shall be based on considerations related to the following potential adverse effects on adjacent properties: Noise, vibration, smoke, particulate matter, odour, toxic matter, fire and explosive hazards, glare, heat and humidity, and electromagnetic interference."[23]

Summary and Conclusions The Victoria Official Regional Plan Industrial section manages to divide the industrial lands of Victoria into areas based on the timeframe for industrial development and develop a comprehensive list of nuisances to be considered when developing new industrial sites. The performance standards for monitoring the adverse conditions listed above would ideally be listed in the industrial section of the Victoria Zoning Bylaw.

2.2.8.2   Victoria Zoning Bylaw 1999

The 1999 Victoria Zoning Bylaw reduces the number of industrial districts from 17. Five districts in the current Zoning bylaw are described below that have direct relevance to the issues present at residential-industrial interfaces.

- **M-1 Zone, Limited Light Industrial District**
    This district resembles the Vancouver MC-1 and MC-2 districts, except for the exclusion of manufacturing, processing and assembly in the Victoria zone. Provision is made for the inclusion of work-live space, which combines residential use (as an accessory use), with any of the permitted indoor uses. The work-live space is located in a unit that is a room or suite of rooms of which not more than 50% of the floor space is used for residential use.

    It is recognized that a segment of the population will want to live in an area that provides an opportunity for flexible living space that can also be used to conduct small-scale business activity. This business will likely be in the form of artisan, studio, or office space.

    The Zoning Bylaw lists the permitted uses allowed in the district, "provided they are not noxious or offensive to any adjacent property or the general public by reason of emitting odours, dust, smoke, gas, noise, effluent, radiation, broadcast interference, glare, humidity, heat, vibration or hazard."[24] This is the similar list of adverse effects of industrial activity encountered in other municipal bylaws. The measurement parameters of these conditions are not included in the zoning bylaw. Height and yard restrictions are also included in the bylaw concerning industrial sites adjacent to predominantly residential areas. "The maximum height of any part of a building within 7.5 m of the internal boundary [of an adjacent predominantly residential district] shall not exceed 4 m."[25] Yards shall be separated from an adjacent residential district "by a landscaped screen of at least 1.5 m in height and 60 cm in width."[26] The Victoria Zoning Bylaw prescribes specific measurements for the size of buildings and intervening screens between incompatible land uses. Finally, a 1 metre landscape berm is required to separate industrial uses from a list of specific streets in Victoria.

- **M-2 Zone, Light Industrial District**
    A slightly reduced list of noxious products of industry are listed for this district, including emitting odours, dust, smoke, gas, noise, effluent, or hazard. The same height and yard restrictions outlined for the M-1 zone apply for the M-2 zone.

- **M2-I Zone, Douglas-Blanshard Industrial District**
  All other M-2 Zone regulations apply to the remainder of this zone. This zone is similar to the M-1 zone except for the inclusion of manufacturing, processing and assembly uses in the zone.

- **M-3 Zone, Heavy Industrial District and S-1 Zone, Limited Service District**
  These zones list the same offensive product, height, and yard rules as the M-2 zone.

Summary and Conclusions Within each description of the industrial zone districts is a provision for the recognition of the production of negative externalities, but there are no specific performance standard regulations written into the bylaw. The bylaw allows for the location of live-work uses in the M-1 zone, and recognizes this particular zone as a more commercial oriented mixed-use area. The inclusion of specific distances and heights for measuring yards and buildings adjacent to residential districts is applied to each industrial zone.

2.2.9 Winnipeg

Winnipeg represents the last city summarized for this section of the report. The recently adopted Winnipeg Plan and the Zoning Bylaw are summarized below.

2.2.9.1 Plan Winnipeg 2001

Plan Winnipeg addresses the industrial interface in the following policies. The purpose of each policy can be found in Appendix K.

- **Implement an Industrial Land Planning Strategy**
  The implementation of the Industrial Land Planning Strategy would identify the level of compatibility of prospective industrial sites with existing residential areas. If designed correctly, this process would ensure that incompatible land use interfaces accompanied by resultant problems are not created.

- **Promote Vibrant Neighbourhoods**
  This policy calls for the development of "light industry at industrial park standards to act as a buffer, where appropriate, between residential development and other incompatible uses."[27] The compatible mixed-uses mentioned could include work-live industrial and residential neighbourhoods. Also, this policy recognizes that industrial park development is an effective buffer between residential areas and heavy industrial uses perceived as producing a greater amount of negative externalities.

- **Accommodating New Industrial Areas**
  Before new industry is developed, the city will ensure existing neighbourhoods are protected. This statement is vague but provides policy support for communities to prevent change from occurring in their community because of new industrial development. The city will also only allow commercial development into industrial areas if the commercial use produces a

buffer effect. The use of commercial uses as a buffer is similar to the strategy applied by Edmonton in the creation of The IB, Industrial Business Zone.

- **Provide Ongoing Stewardship of Industrial Areas**

    Like Edmonton, Calgary, and Ottawa, Winnipeg is interested in protecting the viability of existing industrial areas. Just as residential areas often need protection from the adverse effects produced by industrial neighbours, long standing industrial uses require protection from encroaching residential development.

- **Addresses Water, Air, and Noise Pollution**

    This general statement is found in most municipal plans recognizing the need to protect residential areas from airborne pollutant sources located further afield.

Summary and Conclusions Plan Winnipeg recognizes the importance of protecting the viability of existing industrial areas while simultaneously protecting residential areas from the negative impacts produced by industrial districts. This is oftentimes a difficult task to achieve, particularly in a city such as Winnipeg with a history of industrial use much longer than that of Calgary.

2.2.9.2 Winnipeg Zoning Bylaw

The Zoning Bylaw was established to reflect the vision presented in Plan Winnipeg and other policies based on community goals for the future of the city and its neighborhoods. The city is divided into two regions: Downtown Winnipeg Zoning Bylaw (No. 4800/88) and The City of Winnipeg Zoning Bylaw (No. 6400/94).

According to the City of Winnipeg web site[28], The Downtown Winnipeg Zoning Bylaw does not include the traditional zoning districts that are common in most zoning bylaws. This Bylaw incorporates six separate sets of zoning regulations (or layers), which when combined together form the equivalent of a zoning district with the requirements for that site. Use of this system allows for regulations to be customized for each site. The zoning layers can be found in Appendix K.

Outside the Downtown area, parcels of land are separated into four basic zoning districts: agricultural (A), residential (R), commercial (C) and industrial (M). These categories are further subdivided by the intensity of use, including the industrial zoning district, which is divided into manufacturing categories. Development within these manufacturing districts is governed by use, bulk of the development and parking regulations. The items regulated by each zoning district are listed in Appendix K.

This system closely resembles the standard system of industrial land zoning. Little mention is made of incompatible land use interfaces within the cited summary.

Summary and Conclusions The Winnipeg Zoning Bylaw presents a standard type of land use management in which uses within zones are listed as permitted and lot coverage, parking and signs are regulated. The 2001 Plan Winnipeg does mention the importance of remedying issues at problematic residential-industrial interfaces, and this may translate into a greater inclusion of interface areas in a subsequent zoning bylaw review.

2.3 Canadian Residential-Industrial Interface Policy Matrix

The 10 municipalities examined in this report have been summarized below. Table 2.3 illustrates how each citywide municipal policy, be it the Municipal Plan or Land Use Policy, addresses particular aspects of the residential-industrial interface.

Table 2.3   Canadian Residential-Industrial Interface Policy Matrix

Y- yes, N- no, C- Combined, Z- Zoning Policy Characteristics	Calgary	Edmonton	Hamilton	Ottawa	Regina	Saskatoon	Toronto	Vancouver	Victoria	Winnipeg	Comments
1. Municipal Plan Policy mention of:											
-goal of remedying interface conflicts	Y	Y	■	Y	Y	Y	Y	N	N	Y	-not mentioned in BC policy
-specific interface issues or adverse affects	N	N	■	Y	N	N	Y	N	Y	Y	-plans are often too general to mention specific issues
-need for industrial areas to exist in the city	Y	Y	■	Y	N	Y	Y	Y	Y	Y	-most plans mention goal of keeping older industrial areas in inner city
-industry protection from other land use encroachment	Y	Y	■	Y	N	Y	Y	Y	Y	Y	-most cities see need to keep heavy industry viable; keep homes away
2. Land Use Policy characteristics											
-Development Control or Zoning	C	C	Z	■	Z	Z	■	Z	Z	Z	-Alberta cities only two to not use zoning
-industrial land divided into heavy/light uses	Y	Y	Y	■	Y	Y	■	Y	Y	Y	-Edmonton attempting to implement one zone industrial land use system
-Performance Standards used	Y	Y	N	■	Y	Y	■	Y	Y	Y	-Hamilton document is 22 years old; new policy likely changed
-mention of specific negative externalities	Y	Y	N	■	Y	Y	■	Y	Y	Y	-Hamilton document is 22 years old; new policy likely changed
-landscape requirements addressed	Y	N	N	■	Y	Y	■	N	Y	Y	-often up to scrutiny of approving authority
-protective business policy present	Y	Y	N	■	Y	Y	■	Y	Y	N	-importance of maintaining industry can be codified in the bylaw
-work-live policy present	N	N	N	■	N	N	■	Y	Y	N	-BC cities only
-transitional use districts present	N	Y	N	■	Y	Y	■	Y	Y	N	-the transitional district acts as a buffer zone between uses
-number of Industrial Districts or Zones	4	5	5	■	10	7	■	12	5	■	

The matrix can be used to discern which municipality has mentioned a specific issue associated with the interface in order to direct policy inquiries to that specific policy. In the case where more than one Plan was summarized in the previous sections, the most recently produced document was used in the matrix.

2.4 Conclusion

The Canadian municipalities summarized in this section have addressed the organization of land use regulations according to the particular issues that exist in their jurisdiction. As creatures of their respective provincial governments, municipalities follow models of land use management dictated by provincial legislation. Calgary employs a method of land use management based on zoning and development control, which is unlike the strict zoning style employed by the majority of municipalities listed above. Land use policy is constantly in a state of change, and the review of the Calgary Land Use Bylaw currently underway will result in some form of change to land use regulations that may be subtle or dramatic. Although the industrial land use strategies employed by different cities are unique to their own situations the lessons learned by other cities can be modified and applied to the City of Calgary to create a process of industrial interface land use control that functions better than the current system. Many of the ideas generated by other city industrial interface policy will be considered in the recommendations created in Chapter Five that will attempt to enhance current Calgary residential-industrial interface policy. Up to this point in this report, the history of Canadian and Calgary industrial land use planning has been described and various citywide residential-interface policies for other Canadian municipalities have been summarized. Chapter Three will explain the specific problems that occur at the interfaces that instigate the creation of buffer and transition zone policies.

Notes

[1] Edmonton, 1994.
[2] Edmonton, 2001.
[3] Edmonton, 2001.
[4] Edmonton, 2001.
[5] Edmonton, 2001.
[6] Francisco, Jim, 2002.
[7] Carlston, Jason, 2002.
[8] Regina, 2002.
[9] Regina, 1992.
[10] Regina, 1992.
[11] Regina, 1992.
[12] Regina, 1992.
[13] Saskatoon, 2001.
[14] Saskatoon, 2001.
[15] Saskatoon, 2002.
[16] Saskatoon, 2002.
[17] Saskatoon, 2002.
[18] Vancouver, 2002.
[19] Vancouver, 2002.
[20] Vancouver, 2002.
[21] Vancouver, 2002.
[22] Vancouver, 2002.
[23] Victoria, 1974.
[24] Victoria, 1999.
[25] Victoria, 1999.
[26] Victoria, 1999.
[27] Winnipeg, 2001.
[28] Winnipeg, 2002.

Chapter 3
Problematic Residential-Industrial Interfaces

3.1 What is a Problematic Interface?

The results of industrial land use activity can be deleterious to human and environmental well being. Chapter One illustrates that the effects of industrial activity have permeated city life for nearly 200 years in some parts of the world. The concluding section of the opening chapter and all of Chapter Two explain how some large cities in Canada have attempted to remedy the problems created by placing industry next to incompatible land uses through land use policy. Where industrial land use districts meet other land use districts, the products of industrial activity can adversely affect the adjacent land use. However, it is important to note that the adjacent land uses can also hamper the productivity and quality of the industrial activity. The products of industrial activity have been described in a number of different ways in this report. Terms such as adverse effects, negative externalities, industrial products, and conditions have all been used to describe the phenomena produced at industrial interfaces that may be potentially harmful. The negative externalities produced at the interface can have effects that spread over a large geographical area; some significantly large airborne products of industrial activity can be measured thousands of kilometres from the site. This paper is concerned with conditions that effect adjacent districts only. The places where these potentially harmful phenomena exist at the border with another land use are called problematic interfaces. Specifically, this paper addresses the places where industrial uses border predominantly residential districts; these areas where the different land uses meet are called problematic residential-industrial interfaces.

The Merriam-Webster dictionary defines problematic as: "posing a problem, difficult to solve or decide, not definite or settled, and open to question or debate."[1] All of these definitions describe the situation at many of Calgary's residential-industrial land use interfaces. As a young industrial city, compared with eastern North American industrial centres, Calgary contains many interfaces that are not problematic for people on either side of the interface. The interface does not pose a problem, as the uses on either side may not produce adverse effects for the adjacent district. The interface issues may not be difficult to solve or decide; in some instances the erection of a fence is enough to placate residents whose only concern was an unsightly light industrial business. Often, the imposition of a simple traffic calming measure, like a speed bump, can dissuade people from using an industrial transportation area as a viable shortcut. Not all interfaces are problematic interfaces. In a subsequent section of this report, the residential-industrial interfaces of Calgary will be listed, with the interfaces described as problematic or non-problematic. (The list of all of the communities in Calgary is located in Appendix L). The type of industry or the quality of the barrier established between incompatible land uses can negate possible interface related issues from arising. For example, a high-tech plant with all of its operations conducted within the plant building will be a better neighbour for residents than a rendering plant. Different types of industrial use are better neighbours that others.

Industrial districts border upon non-industrial areas whether the cause is historical evolution or planned land use management. Segregating all industrial uses from other land uses is impossible. Communities have come to realize that "neither distance nor segregation of industry by category would adequately solve all the problems associated with industrial land use."[2] Many industrial uses are required within the city and fulfil smaller scale consumer needs. Industrial uses vary greatly insofar as the scale of the operation, the products created and stored and the type of customer. Industrial uses will continue to exist next to residential districts; the key in ensuring that these two different areas coexist is to:

- place uses next to one another that have no impact on the adjacent district
- create interventions, and an accompanying policy mechanism to initiate intervention strategies, where an incompatible situation does exist.

3.2 The Problematic Phenomena at the Interface

Industry produces phenomena that cause negative externalities for residential districts and residential districts produce activity detrimental to adjacent industry. The following list of off-site impacts is not all encompassing but it represents the majority of documented problems reported by residents and industry. The list was compiled through informal conversations with City of Calgary staff, residents and employees located in the interface area, literature review of municipal policy, the work of Performance Standards expert Jim Schwab, and personal observations. The negative externalities produced by industry and reported by adjacent residents include:

Air Pollution	On Street Parking
Blast Overpressure	Outdoor Storage and Waste Disposal
Broadcast (Electrical) Interference	Particulate Matter
Effluent	Radiation Emissions
Fire and Explosive Hazards	Toxic and Hazardous Materials
Glare	Traffic
Heat and Humidity	Undesirable Social Activity
Litter	Unsightly Properties
Noise	Vibration
Odour	Water Quality Deterioration

Likewise, residential districts produce several problems for adjacent industrial zones, including:

Lodging Unmerited Complaints
On Street Parking
Shortcutting Through Industrial Districts

The negative externalities produced by industry and residences can be measured to describe how the adjacent district is negatively affected. Each phenomenon is characterized by a set of variables that determines the level of nuisance created. Some phenomena are easily measured by simple forms of data collection. Performance standards are then developed to set definite limits as to which levels must be achieved in order for specific uses to be allowed to continue without penalty. Other nuisances were not even known to be problematic until sophisticated technology was developed to measure levels of industrially produced contaminants.

Higher levels of government have regulations in place governing the performance standards of industry. As an example, the Alberta government regulates air pollution levels through the Environmental Protection and Enhancement Act (referred to as the Clean Air Act in the Calgary LUB. The provincial and federal governments tend to regulate the conditions of industry with the greatest potential for harm. Local municipalities usually manage the adverse effects of industrial activity not managed by senior levels of government. This is the most efficient situation because the levels of industrial activity can vary greatly in different municipalities therefore province wide standards for a condition like odour may not adequately control all of the odour problems that can arise in all of Alberta's municipalities. Also, "local governments are often in the best position to promote serious changes in industrial performance precisely because they are the closest governmental link to many small businesses and factories."[3] The negative externalities of industrial and residential districts are described in detail below, including the perceived effect on the adjacent community and how the phenomena are measured according to specified performance standards.

3.2.1   Air Pollution

Any material released into the air can be considered to be air pollution, but this section will deal exclusively with gaseous emissions. At the onset of industrial activity, little was known of the effects of airborne pollutants on adjacent areas. The reasons for this are twofold: first, sufficiently sensitive measuring devices did not exist to measure the by-products of industry and, secondly, the effects of airborne pollutants can be experienced far from the polluter. The effects of chemical pollutants are oftentimes not manifest until chemical processes have occurred at higher levels in the atmosphere, and the negative effects of certain industrial uses may become apparent after the pollutant has travelled thousands of kilometres from the point of origin. Other airborne pollutants, however, do not move far from their source of origin and contribute to local pollution problems like smog. Several of the municipalities identified in Chapter Two, including Toronto and Vancouver, contend with smog related pollution on a daily basis. The immediate airborne discharge of industry can be measured by sophisticated equipment. However, long-term impacts of airborne discharge are difficult to measure. Health impacts, such as significant increases in cancer or birth defect cases next to an industrial site, may not be detectable at a site for generations. The performance standard can only govern whether or not a particular air pollutant is above an acceptable level for a particular point in time. After a number of years of operation, the measurement of increases in health problems adjacent to a site comes far too late for those affected.

The City of Calgary mentions air contaminants as noxious products to be controlled or eliminated at industrial sites. The air contaminant levels are not to exceed those levels prescribed in the Environmental Protection and Enhancement Act (formerly the Clean Air Act). The city may act as an identifier of possible polluters, but enforcement of provincial regulations is the responsibly of the province. The other cities mentioned in Chapter Two also rely on the environmental monitoring division of their provincial governments to control airborne polluters. Inclusion of a performance standard governing air pollution in the land use policy document may be beyond the scope of expertise of smaller municipal administrations. However, including the need to confer with the provincial environmental agency or directing air pollution matters to the provincial regulations is an appropriate inclusion in any land use bylaw. The rules regarding

47

penalties and measurement of the noxious product will be established in the provincial act. Referring to the provincial act in the land use policy document will ensure all interested parties are aware of the regulations to be followed, and who to contact in case an industrial operation at a residential interface is accused of producing harmful airborne pollution.

3.2.2 Blast Overpressure

This term refers to "excess atmospheric pressure generated by blasting operations."[4] A performance standard for this industrial condition would regulate the allowable pressure, in pounds per square inch, produced at the site of a blasting operation. Inclusion of this industrial performance standard would be unnecessary in most municipalities because of the rarity of blasting operations found in urban industrial areas.

3.2.3 Broadcast (Electrical) Interference

The activity of industry can interfere with the quality of television and radio signals attained by adjacent residences. The Victoria Zoning Bylaw mentions this as a negative externality of industry. Industries contributing to broadcast interference are likely unaware of the side effects of their activity. With the proliferation of cable television and radio service, this nuisance would likely be less of a reported problem than it was in previous decades. A local bylaw mentioning this nuisance should refer those contributing to interference to the regulations of the Canadian Radio-Television and Telecommunication Commission.

3.2.4 Effluent

The Merriam-Websters dictionary describes effluent as "waste material (as smoke, liquid industrial refuse, or sewage) discharged into the environment, especially when serving as a pollutant."[5] Smoke is covered in the particulate matter section of this report. Liquid industrial refuse and sewage are perceived to be more polluted than the sewage and waste produced by commercial and residential uses. Provision for the disposal of effluent is little mentioned in the land use regulations of the municipalities covered in Chapter Two. Industrial liquid waste and sewage would likely be managed through a city's wastewater treatment system. Industrial uses are still found to charge rivers and water sources with untreated waste products. Monitoring of effluent levels is similar to air pollution in that the effects of the pollution are experienced a long distance from the site of origin if transported by a waterway. Control of effluent levels is within provincial jurisdiction and should be mentioned as such within the performance standards section of municipal land use policy.

3.2.5 Fire and Explosive Hazards

Fire and explosive hazards are two of the more dangerous effects of an unplanned industrial discharge event for adjacent residential areas. The Hub Oil event described at the onset of this report describes how a community can be effected when fire and explosions occur at an industrial compound. Municipal fire departments should be able to provide communities with the expertise needed to devise solutions and appropriate standards for the storage of flammable, explosive, and reactive chemicals. Including the management of specific materials in a land use policy might be too difficult to manage. Firstly, planners are not trained to recognize the properties of fire and explosive threats. Secondly, chemical storage methods change regularly, and the land use policy would require constant revision and amendment to keep up with changes in technology. The best method for managing the storage of flammable, explosive, or reactive chemicals is to rely on the skills of the fire department and refer to the fire safety regulations within the land use policy. The Calgary LUB refers to the Fire Prevention Bylaw as the source for information regarding the management of these chemicals. Concurrent with the creation of this paper is the creation of a Calgary Fire Department report addressing changes and additions to the LUB related to the placement of potentially hazardous occupancies in relation to residential communities.

3.2.6 Glare

Alternatively known as light pollution, glare is excess light produced to the detriment of adjacent uses. Other cities refer to glare as a high brightness light source. Industrial operations running under intense light at night can cause a problem for adjacent residents attempting to sleep. Sometimes critical to operation during evening hours, the glare can be shielded in order to diminish its effect on adjacent sleepers. The light is often intensified to function as a deterrent to criminal activity occurring on site. Glare is a negative externality that is comparatively straightforward to control. A performance standard concerning glare could "specify that all lighting must be shielded so as to prevent excessive off-site illumination or meet a specific standard for luminescence."[6] Turning off or dimming lights through the installation of light shields can drastically reduce the problem.

3.2.7 Heat and Humidity

Traditionally, heat and humidity are products of heavy industrial uses and are rarely located next to residential areas. Large-scale smelters, metal production operations, and other heat and humidity producers could erect heat barriers on site boundaries to minimize impacts on adjacent industrial uses.

3.2.8 Litter

Litter is produced when waste or materials stored at industrial sites is transported off site and deposited in an improper manner or place. Material used in industrial production blown by wind can collect on adjacent properties, producing significant accumulations of industrial wastes. The types of waste can range from paper packaging products found at almost all industrial sites to animal parts improperly disposed of at animal processing operations. Materials that accumulate on vehicles at industrial sites can become dislodged in adjacent areas, leaving mud,

Chapter 3- Problematic Residential-Industrial Interfaces

dust, and industrial chemicals on roadways. Ensuring that materials are properly stored and sheltered from the wind on industrial sites and that vehicle cleaning facilities are located on industrial sites can be included in municipal regulations.

3.2.9   Noise

Noise is one of the most widely reported complaints by residents living adjacent to industrial areas. The average human responses to sound levels are outlined in Appendix B along with information about the City of Calgary noise bylaw. Municipalities initiate noise bylaws that limit the amount of noise, measured as a decibel level that can be produced by businesses, residents, and equipment. The noise measuring equipment is effective at monitoring noises that persist over a long period of time. Intermittent noises, however, are difficult to monitor and regulate and are oftentimes not recognized by measurement equipment. Industrial manufacturing activity can produce loud noise pulses at regular intervals, which can be a much greater nuisance for adjacent residents than a continuous noise at a higher decibel level. Noise in the evening is often perceived to be more of a nuisance than the same amount of noise produced during the day. Municipalities often adopt different thresholds of noise allowance for the evening hours than for the regular business day. As one of the greatest nuisances facing residents adjacent to industrial sites, most bylaws also include at least a mention of the municipal noise bylaw, and some may include a brief summary of the noise bylaw within the land use policy document. However, "industrial noise has taken a back seat in recent years to other sources [of noise], including urban traffic, construction, and airport operations."[7] Noise bylaws also try to control noise produced by these other sources. Solutions for communities experiencing unacceptable levels of industry produced noise include restricting industrial operations at certain times of day and the erection of noise attenuation walls.

3.2.10   Odour

Aside from noise, little raises the ire of residents more than malodorous emanations from industrial sites. Also like noise, "odour tends to be a local problem, best managed through local standards."[8] Odours are released through the manipulation of chemicals, or originate from materials stored on industrial sites. "Performance standards are particularly effective in targeting stationary sources of odours, such as improperly stored or decaying materials or poorly controlled chemical reactions."[9] A human investigator can measure odour, but wind patterns and production schedules can dramatically alter the day-to-day spread of odour limiting the effectiveness of an investigator who measures the odour on a windless day of limited industrial production. Measuring devices can be used to quantify odour, but in municipalities with infrequent odour complaints, the nuisance can be managed by a diligent investigator.

3.2.11   On Street Parking

Industrial districts can be deficient in meeting civic parking standards. This can be the result of insufficient parking regulations, limited enforcement, and industrial business expansion not accompanied by parking expansion. Industrial districts are often underserved by public transit and large operations can function in the evening and morning hours when public transit service is suspended or significantly reduced; industrial employees must therefore drive to work. Industrial enterprises that operate through the evening can produce a shortage of on street parking spaces in adjacent residential districts where the street functions as a local parking area in the evening. Parking restrictions in the form of permit only parking areas maintain the use of the street as a residential parking area but do not address the parking needs of local business.

3.2.12 Outdoor Storage and Waste Disposal

The inadequate disposal of waste and the improper storage of material may not only produce odours and chemical pollution, but may attract vermin and pests. Disease can spread to nearby people and wildlife as a result of the spread of some improperly disposed of material. Dust and airborne pollutants can be unleashed from substances loosely stored outdoors. Wind can blow these pollutants into adjacent neighbourhoods and further afield (a situation especially true for Calgary). Potentially harmful material can be stored in transport vehicles on industrial sites. It would be difficult for land use policy to limit the type of materials transported to certain industrial sites, however land use policy could limit the type of vehicles that could be stored on site or the size of vehicle that could use certain roadways. Periodic inspections are the method used to ensure adequate storage and improper disposal methods are being employed in accordance with municipal regulations. These rules may be included in the list of industrial performance standards.

3.2.13 Particulate Matter

Particulate matter is not only detrimental to air quality, but the airborne pollutants can accelerate the degradation of both natural and built environments through erosion, discolouration, and death to trees and wildlife. The release of particulate matter is one of the more conspicuous by-products of industrial activity. The visual appearance of plumes and the smell accompanying the material is difficult to ignore. Again, the regulation of particle emissions is pursuant to the rules of the Environmental Protection and Enhancement Act in Alberta.

3.2.14 Radiation Emissions

Only Edmonton mentions radiation as an emission to be monitored and controlled a performance standard. Organizations require a license for the possession and use of radioactive materials which is granted by the Atomic Energy Control Board.[10] It would be a rarity for most industrial operations to store or handle radioactive material in an urban industrial site. The scale of the petroleum processing operations in Edmonton and vicinity call for the inclusion of this noxious condition.

3.2.15 Toxic and Hazardous Materials

Within this category are included materials that are described as hazardous by a regulating organization. Toxic and hazardous materials can present serious health, safety, fire, and pollution risks to the site, the adjacent areas, and to the region depending upon the type of material located on site and the release event. The single incident involving a leak of "methyl isocyanante (MIC) from a Union Carbide plant lead 1000s of deaths and injuries from the inhalation of toxic fumes."[11] If handled properly, there is no reason, outside of a cataclysmic triggering event like a natural disaster that would cause toxic and hazardous materials to be threatening. However, when improperly stored and handled the possibility of risk increases and the presence of these materials on industrial sites becomes much more hazardous. Potentially dangerous chemicals handled carefully and properly are less of a threat to people than less dangerous chemicals handled in an imprudent manner.

The City of Calgary Fire Department is currently re-examining how commercial handlers of toxic and hazardous materials report the lists and quantities of materials stored on business sites. The storage of some materials is inappropriate for some communities. Certain materials, although they may be handled within safety parameters, are unfit for handling adjacent to residential areas. "It is entirely possible for a community to decide that some substances are simply inappropriate in certain districts, in which case prohibiting their storage or use would be a sensible response."[12] Municipal planning agencies should not be expected to govern the inventory of the presence of these materials but specific land uses known to store or use specific chemicals can be restricted from locating at interfaces. A list of these uses developed by MIACC can be found in Appendix M. There should be mention in the land use policy of materials that are expressly prohibited form locating in a specific land use district, or reference to the Fire Department or responsible agency guidelines for the storage of specific chemicals.

3.2.16 Traffic

Industrial districts can produce an influx of heavy truck traffic into a community. The problems associated with traffic shortcutting include an increase in air pollution in the form of heavy truck exhaust, a decrease in the safety level of pedestrian crossings, and the deterioration of roads not designed for heavy load transport. Traffic issues are best measured through traffic counts and participant observation. Interventions, such as declaring no-truck routes, recalculating speed limits, and installing impediments designed to make the short cut an undesirable route can be employed to remove industrial traffic from the residential zone.

3.2.17 Undesirable Social Activity

Little recognized in the literature, industrial areas that operate during daylight hours and are therefore virtually abandoned at night could become popular sites for conducting illegal or dangerous activity. Busy industrial sites during the day can become the focus of prostitution and drug trafficking activity at night. Some industrial districts deserted in the evening can become the sites for a variety of other non-traditional activities like streetcar racing and gambling. The large size of industrial sites may make them attractive to criminals. This activity can spill over into adjacent residential neighbourhoods. This would not be covered in a performance standard and would be the responsibility of the local police department and landowner. However, planners can employ the precepts of crime prevention through environmental design (CPTED) to create an environment unfavourable for criminal activity.

3.2.18   Unsightly Properties

Even when an industry produces no measurable condition that affects the adjacent residential community, the site and building may be in such disrepair and in such a neglected state that a perceived decrease in the quality of the community and property value results. Landscape and buffer regulations are employed in many municipalities to ensure residents are shielded from unattractive storage yards and parking areas. Storage regulations can be used to control what materials are stored on site and to ensure certain visually inappropriate products are stored indoors. Soft landscaping, in the form of vegetation like trees and shrubs, and hard landscaping, like fences and walls, can screen residences from storage yards. Hard dividers are most often used where other noxious conditions impact an adjacent housing district. A concrete wall will not only block the sight of the property but can deflect noise produced on site. However, soft landscape options can provide a more attractive solution for screening unsightly properties. Combining a raised berm and soft landscaping is, if the intervening land is available for such a project, produce the most visually pleasant land use buffer.

3.2.19   Vibration

Earthborne vibrations are the result of operating heavy vibrating equipment. High intensity vibrations can disrupt activity of neighbouring facilities and cause structural damage to adjacent structures, including homes and other industrial buildings. Equipment exists to measure the displacement of particles during a vibration event. Vibration equipment is not commonly found in lighter industrial areas, and limiting the use of such equipment to heavy industrial areas will minimize the problem.

3.2.20   Water Quality Deterioration

Industrial areas are located next to flowing water and sites of water accumulation. Ponds and lakes can be situated next to industrial sites or located fully within industrial areas. This water is often used as a source of plant water and power. As mentioned above, running water can be the terminal point for waste material produced at industrial sites. The by-products of industrial activity can also affect the quality and quantity of groundwater as well. Water quality is another noxious effect of industrial activity that may not necessarily affect adjacent districts. However, groundwater contamination can affect adjacent districts by transporting potentially hazardous substances in the groundwater. Potentially harmful industrial by-products can be emptied into city constructed water carriers, including storm and wastewater sewage systems. The performance standards concerning sewer and natural watercourse outflow and groundwater are normally not mentioned in land use policy. Clarity would be ensured if reference to provincial government regulation was included in the land use policy regarding water quality.

Residential districts can cause problems for adjacent industry, including:

3.2.21 Lodging Unmerited Complaints

Being situated next to an industrial district can be perceived in a negative light by residents located at the interface and those nowhere near the interface. Residents can lodge complaints concerning the potentially negative by-products of industrial activity even though they live beside an industry that does not transgress any bylaw and acts as a problem free neighbour. Perception of a problem does not make a problem. Each complaint lodged by a resident must be addressed by the appropriate official to ensure the complaint has merit. Just as residential zones should expect certain activity constraints placed upon adjacent industrial uses, industrial businesses should be assured that if they follow the rules and are legally entitled to conduct business at their location, then they should be able to do so without disturbance.

3.2.22 On Street Parking

On street parking in industrial areas is often required for delivery vehicles on a short-term basis. Uses in residential areas, including churches, schools, and playing fields may not have sufficient parking, and these people may park in adjacent industrial districts, blocking possible parking spaces for transport vehicles. Limiting the on street parking to loading zones for commercial uses would limit this disruptive traffic behaviour.

3.2.23 Shortcutting through Industrial Districts

Just as industrial traffic can disrupt traffic patterns in residential areas, residential traffic in industrial areas can disrupt the flow of heavy vehicle traffic in industrial zones. Industrial districts include warehousing and distribution centre uses that require hassle free access and egress to the industrial site. Non-industrial vehicle use of these transportation routes can increase the difficulty for heavy vehicles to effectively conduct their business.

Summary and Conclusions Not all of the 23 negative externalities listed above occur in Calgary. Many of these conditions are indicative of heavier industry and are sufficiently shielded from incompatible land uses by lower intensity industrial districts. No industrial use will produce every nuisance listed above. However, certain uses can produce nuisances in combination that can be problematic for the adjacent residential area. Likewise, the residentially produced nuisances can compound into larger issues for industrial areas.

3.3 Groupings of Negative Externalities

The 23 adverse effects listed above can be separated into groups according to their levels of impact on adjacent districts. These groupings of negative externalities will be used to categorize the communities of Calgary according to the type of conditions present at the industrial interface. The communities located adjacent to the industrial interfaces containing Group 1 negative externalities will be described in greater detail in Chapter Four.

3.3.1 Group 1: High-Risk Negative Externalities

The first category includes all of the conditions that have the potential to create a short-term or long-term health hazard and may produce a significant disaster situation involving risk to the safety of neighbouring districts including the possibility of evacuation. The conditions present at industrial interfaces that pose the greatest risk for adjacent residential districts include:

Air pollution	Particulate Matter
Effluent	Radiation Emissions
Fire and Explosive Hazards	Toxic and Hazardous Materials
Outdoor Storage and Waste Disposal	Water Quality Deterioration

These negative externalities are traditionally products of heavy industrial activity and are typically monitored by provincial or federal levels of government. The by-products of these negative externalities can result in a risk to human life and the environment.[=] Several of these conditions can spread beyond the adjacent districts, but the report is concerned only with directly adjacent interface areas.

3.3.2 Group 2: Nuisance-Only Negative Externalities

These negative externalities can cause significant problems for effected people but the condition will not result in a risk to human life in most circumstances. Italics denote a negative externality produced by a residential district.

Blast Overpressure	On Street Parking
Broadcast Interference	*On Street Parking by Industry*
Glare	*Shortcutting Through Industrial Districts*
Heat and Humidity	Traffic
Litter	Undesirable Social Activity
Lodging Unmerited Complaints	Unsightly Properties
Noise	Vibration
Odour	

[=] The use of the word risk is not to be confused with the idea of Risk as used by MIACC.

Traffic accidents, run-ins with criminals and vibration damage can all lead to injury, death or property damage but this paper emphasizes the nuisance qualities of these conditions that can be managed through land use policy.

Summary and Conclusions Some types of interface conditions have the potential to impact human life greater than others do. The division into two groups of interfaces can be used to create a classification of geographic areas in need of particular types of policy interventions. The following section of the report will illustrate where the industrial areas of Calgary are situated, and lead into a further description of where residential-industrial interfaces proliferate.

3.4 The Industrial Areas of Calgary

Figure 3.1 shows all of the current and potential industrial areas in Calgary over the course of the 2000-2004 planning period.[13] Many of the industrial edges identified on the map have yet to be developed. Aside from the central industrial area and the University research park, the other industrial areas are not completely surrounded by other land uses.

Many of the older pockets of industrial activity have been relocated to other areas on the periphery of the City. Figure 3.1 illustrates that the City has made a concerted effort to cluster industrial activity into larger industrial areas. Small pockets of sites designated for Industrial use exist throughout the city but these areas are not included in this examination. Many of these sites have been converted to non-industrial uses and redesignation to another land use is, in most cases, inevitable. Problematic residential-industrial interfaces do exist at these sites, but the recommendations of this report will be presented at a district wide scale. The recommendations could be used to remedy land use incompatibility issues arising at the scale of the individual lot.

Calgary's industry can be divided into three large zones of industrial activity:

- The central zone is located close to the City's downtown and is the oldest functioning industrial area in the City. There is little room for growth and expansion in this area as it is surrounded by development on all sides. The major north-south CPR line and MacLeod Trail bisect this area.

- The north-northeast industrial area has, at its core, the International Airport. Expansion in this industrial area is possible to the north and northeast.

- The southeast industrial area is the site of the most intensive industrial activity in Calgary, ranging from warehousing, storage, manufacturing, and limited servicing miscellaneous activity. Included in this industrial zone are the Ogden Shops, one of the oldest rail oriented industrial area in Calgary.

Figure 3.1- The Industrial Areas of Calgary

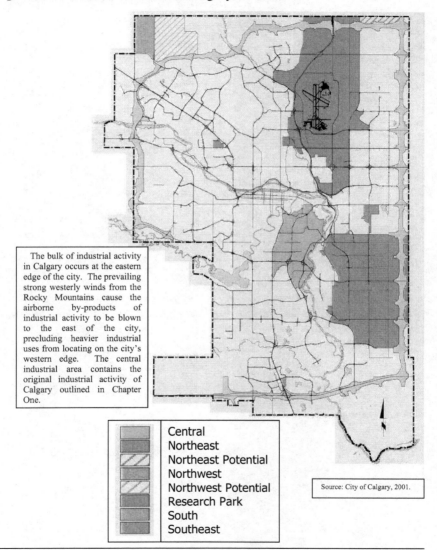

The bulk of industrial activity in Calgary occurs at the eastern edge of the city. The prevailing strong westerly winds from the Rocky Mountains cause the airborne by-products of industrial activity to be blown to the east of the city, precluding heavier industrial uses from locating on the city's western edge. The central industrial area contains the original industrial activity of Calgary outlined in Chapter One.

Central
Northeast
Northeast Potential
Northwest
Northwest Potential
Research Park
South
Southeast

Source: City of Calgary, 2001.

3.5 Residential-Industrial Interfaces in Calgary by Community

The following four maps show Calgary divided into the quadrant system used to demarcate street and avenue numbers in the city. Industrial areas appear in blue and non-industrial areas appear in white. For a complete list of the abbreviated communities of Calgary, refer to Appendix L. The maps are from the City of Calgary website.

Figure 3.2- Northwest Quadrant Residential-Industrial Interfaces

Figure 3.3- Northeast Quadrant Residential-Industrial Interfaces

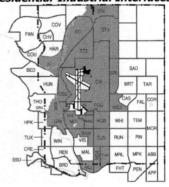

Figure 3.4- Southwest Quadrant Residential-Industrial Interfaces

Figure 3.5- Southeast Quadrant Residential-Industrial Interfaces

3.6 Interface Features by Residential Community

The previous 4 maps show the residential communities in Calgary located adjacent to industrial areas. As described previously, the interfaces where these seemingly incompatible land uses meet are not all problematic. There are residential communities that abut industrial districts where there exists a sufficient space, barrier, or other feature between the two areas that nullifies potential problems between the land use districts. Examples of these features include:

> Water feature
> Transportation route
> Berm
> Fence
> Park or open space
> Another land use district

Many of these features are used in combination. Each of these features is described below.

3.6.1 Water Feature

Rivers are typically located in most major industrial municipalities, and they can oftentimes act as barriers between different land uses. Not only does the stream channel itself divide land, but also the regulations governing development on a riverbed floodplain can limit the scale and type of development near the river's edge. Historically, riverfronts, lakefronts and ocean edges were desirable sites of industrial activity. The water produced power for the operation of the industry, a transportation route, and a convenient place to dispose of waste. In the Calgary context, the Bow River valley was a traditional location for industry, as the railway was built along the river course. The Central industrial area is sandwiched between the Bow and Elbow Rivers, and the rivers separate these industrial areas from adjacent residential areas. The width of the floodplain combined with the lack of accessibility across the river channels limits issues arising at these interfaces.

3.6.2 Transportation Route

A transportation route is describes any type of road, railway, or transportation right-of-way. The activities of the transportation route can produce adverse affects for adjacent residences rivaling the worst industrial operations. Roads separating industry form residential districts can range from gravel alleys, as found in Greenview and Fairview, to major highways like the Deerfoot Trail. The constant noise and exhaust produced by vehicles along major roads adversely affect residential areas in Calgary, and often lead to the construction of sound attenuation barriers. The Light Rail Transit (LRT) and railway routes also divide incompatible uses. The LRT vehicles themselves are low noise producers, but the noise and light produced at stations and road crossings is significant. The railway has been a constant fixture in Calgary, and industrial uses still locate next to the tracks in Ramsay and Inglewood. The rail lines act as a moving industrial site as rail cars store any type of imaginable product. The rail companies have little responsibility insofar as disclosing which materials are transported along the rail lines. The potential for risk produced by a rail accident or leak can be far greater than that produced by stationery industrial sites. Rail rights-of-way are only briefly mentioned in this report; an examination of the problematic rail interfaces would fall under the scope of a wholly independent report.

3.6.3 Berm

Berms are raised mounds of earth used to visually shield incompatible land uses from one another. Typically, the mound would be covered with grass and assorted vegetation and placed on the residential side of the interface. Berms provide a visually appealing separation between land uses but often, if built to a significant height, require a significantly wide tract of land.

3.6.4 Fence

Fences are often built after issues of incompatibility continue at a land use interface. Fences can range form chain link fences designed only to keep people out of a site to tall noise attenuation walls designed to direct noise and other airborne pollutants form an adjacent area. Fences can be employed as interventions along interfaces where the unsightly appearance of industrial areas continues as an issue for adjacent residents. The fence may only act as an interim measure along interfaces where more land use policy controls are required.

3.6.5 Park or Open Space

Where adequate land is available, tracts of open space or parks function as ideal buffers. Golf courses, naturalized urban park areas, and agricultural uses all provide separation distance between homes and industry. Playing fields located on the residential-industrial interface can provide recreational opportunities for residents and industrial district employees in recreationally undeserved areas. Even small-scale pocket parks and playgrounds, if adequately landscaped, can provide a sufficient buffer. As stressed above, the perception of having industrial neighbours can be far worse than the actual probability of any problems arising. Softening the interface between the two districts can ease communities' suspicions about their industrial neighbours, especially if the industry takes an active role in building the interface park.

3.6.6 Another Land Use District

Commercial malls and institutional uses are placed between incompatible land uses. However, these other land uses may produce greater problems for these perceived incompatible neighbours. Commercial uses located along major roads attract heavy volumes of traffic and, depending on the business, activity in evening hours. This increase in traffic can have parking and shortcutting implications on adjacent residential and industrial areas. An industrial business park operating on standard office hours can be an exemplary neighbour for a residential area compared to a strip mall containing a service station, restaurant, and convenience store that are open at all hours.

As mentioned above, the industrial land use itself may prove a model neighbour for residential districts. Many of the uses within a typical light industrial land use category are appropriate neighbours for residential areas. The key to successful residential-industrial interface management is controlling which land uses are appropriate to locate close to residences. The following charts outline the residential-industrial interfaces in Calgary. The interface condition is described, along with the Land Use Designation and actual use located (where possible) on either side of the interface. The definitions for the abbreviations used in the chart can be found in Appendix N.

Table 3.1- Residential-Industrial Interfaces in Northwest Calgary

Community District	Use at Edge	LUD	Interface Feature	LUD	Use at Edge	Industrial District
Country Hills	Park	A/PE	West Nose Creek	DC		Huntington Hills BP
Royal Oak	Agriculture	PE	112 Av NW	UR/PS	Reservoir	Research & Devt. Park
Uni. Of Calgary	Parking	PS	32 Av NW	UNR		U of C Research Park
Varsity		R-1	37 St NW	UNR		U of C Research Park

Table 3.2- Residential-Industrial Interfaces in Northeast Calgary

Community District	Use at Edge	LUD	Interface Feature	LUD	Use	Industrial District
Beddington Heights	SFD	R-1	Beddington Tr	UR		Huntington Hills BP
Castleridge	SFD	R-1	Castleridge Bv NE	DC/PE		Westwinds
Coventry Hills	Parks/SFD	PE/R-1	CP line	UR		Stoney Industrial
Falconridge	SFD	C1-A	Falconridge Bv NE	C-5		Westwinds
Greenview	Townhouses	RM-4	Pasture	A		Skyline West
	Townhouses	RM-4	Pasture	A		Greenview Industrial Park
Harvest Hills	SFD	DC/R-2	96 Av NE	DC/UR		Huntington Hills BP
	SFD	A/R1-A	CP line	UR		Stoney Industrial
Highland Park	SFD	R-2	1 St NE/34 Av NE	I-2		Greenview Industrial Park
Huntington Hills	SFD	PE/UR	Deerfoot Tr	I-2/UR		Deerfoot Business Centre
Marlborough	Commercial	DC	36 St NE	DC/I-2	Mall	Franklin
Martindale	SFD	DC	44 St NE	DC/PE		Saddle Ridge Industrial
Mayland Heights		PE/RM-4	Park	I-2		Mayland Industrial
	SFD	R-2	Barlow Tr NE	I-2		Meridian
	Commercial	C-6	16 Av	DC		South Airways
Rundle	Townhouses	DC	36 St NE	DC/PS	Mall	Sunridge
Thorncliffe	SFD	R-1	Pasture	A		Skyline West
Vista Heights	Park	A/PE	Park	DC/I-2		South Airways
Whitehorn	SFD	R-1/R-2	36 St NE	I-2		Horizon
	SFD	UR	McKnight Bv NE	I-2		Westwinds
Winston Hts/MV	Park/SFD	PE/R-2	34 Av NE	I-2		Greenview Industrial Park

61

Chapter 3- Problematic Residential-Industrial Interfaces

Table 3.3- Residential-Industrial Interfaces in Southwest Calgary

Community District	Use at Edge	LUD	Interface Feature	LUD	Use	Industrial District
Erlton	Park	PE	MacLeod Tr	PE		Manchester Industrial
Kingsland	Commercial	C-6	MacLeod Tr	C-3		Fairview Industrial
Manchester		DC	LRT line	I-2		Manchester Industrial
Meadowlark Park	Commercial	C-6	MacLeod Tr	C-3		Manchester Industrial
Parkhill/Stanley Park	Commercial	C-3	MacLeod Tr	C-3		Manchester Industrial

Table 3.4- Residential-Industrial Interfaces in Southeast Calgary

Community District	Use at Edge	LUD	Interface Feature	LUD	Use	Industrial District
Acadia	SFD	R-1/R-2	Blackfoot Tr SE	DC		East Fairview Industrial
Albert Park/ Radisson Heights	Townhouses	DC/PE	Memorial Dr	I-2		Mayland
	Townhouses	DC/PE	Memorial Dr	DC/I-2		Meridian
	Townhouses	DC	Memorial Dr	I-2		Franklin
Douglas Glen	SFD	DC/R-1	24 St SE	DC		Shepard Industrial
Douglasdale	SFD	R-1	Deerfoot Tr	DC/I-2		Shepard Industrial
Dover		DC/PE	CN line	DC		Forest Lawn Industrial
		R-1	CN line	I-4		Golden Triangle
		R-1	Peigan Tr SE	I-2		Valleyfield
Erin Woods	SFD	R-2/RM-1	Erin Woods Dr SE	I-2	retail	Forest Lawn Industrial
	Mobile homes	DC/UR	35 St SE	I-2		Golden Triangle
		R-2	Peigan Tr. SE	I-2		Eastfield
Fairview	SFD	PE/R-1	Back alley	I-2		Fairview Industrial
Forest Lawn	Townhouses	RM-4	48 St SE	DC/I-2		Forest Lawn Industrial
Inglewood	SFD	DC/R-2	Residential streets	I-2		Alyth/Bonnybrook
McKenzie Tn.	SFD	DC	Pasture	DC		East Shepard Industrial
Ogden		C-3/R-2	Ogden Rd SE	I-3	rail	Ogden Shops
	Mobile Homes	DC/UR	Glenmore Tr SE	I-2/I-3/UR		South Foothills
Penbrooke		C-3/R-1	17 Av SE	DC/C-6		Forest Lawn Industrial
Ramsay	SFD	R-2	Residential streets	I-2		Alyth/Bonnybrook
Red Carpet		C-6	17 Av SE	DC/UR		Forest Lawn Industrial
Riverbend		DC	24 St SE	UR		South Foothills
Sundance	SFD	R-2	Sunpark Dr SE	DC(I-2)		Sundance BP

3.7 Towards a Typology of Problematic Interfaces

Tables 3.1-3.4 list the 41 communities that, at least in part, border an adjacent industrial district. Many of the interfaces pose no problems for the residential or industrial districts. The interface condition or industrial activity is such that the land uses at the interface are compatible. However, there are interface areas rife with problems because of the incompatible arrangement of industrial and residential land uses. The communities listed above in the tables will be further divided into three interface typology categories, including non-problematic interfaces, nuisance-only interfaces, and the most problematic interfaces.

The criteria used to decide how to organize the communities include:

- Figure 3.6, Residences within 200 metres of Industrial Land
- The quality of the interface condition as noted in participant observation field studies
- Incidents of reported problems by City of Calgary staff

3.7.1   Residences within 200 metres of Industrial Land

A map showing the residential areas of Calgary located within 200 metres of an industrial land use is shown in figure 3.6. The 200-metre contour showed the greatest detail without excessive clutter appearing on the map.

Figure 3.6- Residential Land Use within 200 metres of Industrial Land Use

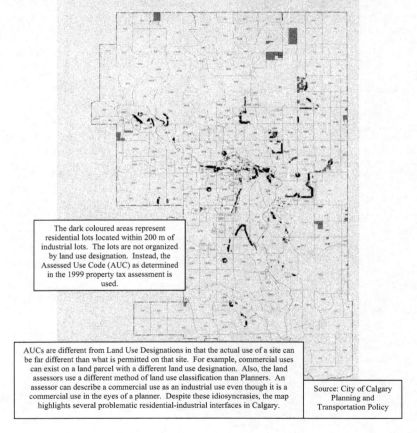

The dark coloured areas represent residential lots located within 200 m of industrial lots. The lots are not organized by land use designation. Instead, the Assessed Use Code (AUC) as determined in the 1999 property tax assessment is used.

AUCs are different from Land Use Designations in that the actual use of a site can be far different than what is permitted on that site. For example, commercial uses can exist on a land parcel with a different land use designation. Also, the land assessors use a different method of land use classification than Planners. An assessor can describe a commercial use as an industrial use even though it is a commercial use in the eyes of a planner. Despite these idiosyncrasies, the map highlights several problematic residential-industrial interfaces in Calgary.

Source: City of Calgary Planning and Transportation Policy

There are some areas included on the map above that are not mentioned in this report. Pocket industrial sites within residential districts have not been described. This leads to the discrepancies between figures 3.2-3.5 and the table above. Figures 3.2 to 3.5 on page 11 include areas already delineated as industrial, even though the areas are undeveloped. A large portion of the northwest corner is planned as a research and development park even though no such activity occurs there at this time. Figure 3.6 shows a significant amount of residences within 200 metres of industrial activity in the community of Bowness, in northwest Calgary. Bowness is a long established community and existed as an independent town before amalgamated by Calgary in 1961. As an independent town, Bowness was the site of industrial activity along the rail line that bisects the community. Several parcels remain as industrial districts, although manufacturing and assembly light industrial activities would encroach on many neighbouring homes. Most of the business activity in the Bowness community is now of a commercial or retail nature, even though areas are still designated as I-2. Other pocket industrial areas exist around the city, usually in historically industrial areas that have changed to a new use. For example, most of the sites assessed as industrial along the CP rail line in the downtown are commercial or office uses. Another anomalous area is located in Sunnyside, located just north of downtown on the map. A land use assessed as industrial creates a ring of residences on the western edge of the community. The land use in question is a garage structure located beside the LRT tracks. The building is within a residential land use district, contains vehicle storage and assorted other uses, and is assessed as industrial. The interface is non-problematic but still appears on the map. The map is not an absolute indicator of problematic residential-industrial interfaces.

However, other interfaces known by residents, businessmen, and city staff to be problematic are well defined on the map. The Fairview, Erin Woods, Forest Lawn, Vista Heights, Mayland Heights, and Highland Park industrial interfaces are all well defined as distinct lines on the map. The Inglewood and Ramsay interface is not as linear as the other interface areas because these two communities are located in the area where industry began in Calgary. This area is characterized by industrial uses intermingled with residences before the advent of land use designation in Calgary. All of the communities to be identified as existing at a significant problematic industrial interface appear in figure 3.6.

3.7.2 The Quality of the Interface Condition

Several excursions were conducted into all of the interface areas. Participant observation was used to note the odour, noise, traffic and parking produced at the interfaces. Overall impressions of the visual appearance of the interfaces were noted and compared with those observations of other who have experience in the interface areas, from residents to those who work in these areas. These observations were noted informally and acted to reinforce conclusions made by the researcher. Extensive forays into the interface areas did not identify any new interface areas not found on figure 3.6. The observations did aid in eliminating interfaces from consideration as being most problematic.

3.7.3 Incidents of Reported Problems by City of Calgary Staff

Informal conversations were held with other Planners and Aldermanic Assistants to confirm the observations noted during field excursions. The interfaces recognized as problematic by the researcher were mentioned by Aldermanic Assistants as sources of complaints. The conversations with other staff, local residents and businesspeople were always held in an informal setting and the results of these conversations were only used to confirm the observations of the researcher in developing the three category interface typologies. The specifics of the conversations or individual observations will not be used in this paper. It is important to note that the observations of others only augmented the researcher's understanding of which interfaces were more problematic than others. Ultimately, the interface typology is the creation of the researcher alone.

3.8 The Problematic Residential-Industrial Interface Typology

The 41 communities listed in tables 3.2-3.5 will be divided into three different categories. The first category will include communities located at an industrial interface where no problems attributed to the industrial or residential use exist. The problems created by the presence of other intermediary uses have not been considered. Potential buffer commercial districts are not included in this report; only problems directly attributed to the industry or residential district are considered. Category two includes communities located at an interface characterized by Group 2 negative externalities. The problems are real, but the issues are of a day-to-day nuisance level, including noise, odour, and unsightly properties. The final category will include communities located next to Group 1 negative externalities, where a significant threat exists for a land use district because of the activity of the other land use district. This can include life threatening adverse effects such as the production of airborne pollutants to the proliferation of unsafe traffic. The communities are sorted by category below.

3.8.1 Category 1: Non-Problematic Residential-Industrial Interfaces

Some of the communities on Calgary's periphery experience no industrial interface problems because the industrial areas have yet to be developed. Problems may potentially arise over time leading to a recategorization of these communities. Other communities have sufficient interface interventions in place that the effects of negative externalities are not experienced. Still other comminutes are located next to industries that produce no measurable adverse effects. The category 1 communities are:

Acadia	Falconridge	Meadowlark Park	Rundle
Beddington Heights	Harvest Hills	Parkhill/Stanley Pk.	Sundance
Coventry Hills	Huntington Hills	Red Carpet	Thorncliffe
Douglas Glen	Kingsland	Riverbend	U. of Calgary
Douglasdale	Marlborough	Royal Oak	Varsity
Erlton	McKenzie Towne		

3.8.2 Category 2: Nuisance Only Residential-Industrial Interfaces

As the uses at interfaces change or the management of those uses changes, the communities in this category may be moved to a different category. The use of a recommended intervention presented in chapter 5 may change an interface into a non-problematic interface. The community and associated interface issues appear below.

Table 3.5   Nuisance Only Residential-Industrial Interfaces

Community	Nuisances Occurring at the Interface
Albert Park/Radisson Heights	Glare, Noise, Odour, Traffic
Castleridge	Noise, Odour, Litter, Traffic
Country Hills	Noise
Greenview	Noise, Unsightly Properties, Traffic
Martindale	Odour, Unsightly Properties
Mayland Heights	Noise, Traffic
Penbrooke	Noise, Odour, Unsightly Properties
Whitehorn	Noise, Odour

3.8.3 Category 3: The Most Problematic Residential-Industrial Interfaces

These interfaces require the most significant level of intervention in order to remedy existing problems for industry and residences. The potential for injury and damage exists at these interfaces because of the proximity of homes to adjacent incompatible industrial land uses.

Every problematic edge is located east of Centre Street, in areas of the city that have been developed for at least 30 years, and, in may cases, much longer. The Area Redevelopment Plans of several of these communities will be summarized in the following chapter to better understand how community scale land use policy has been written to mitigate long standing land use interface concerns of communities and adjacent industry.

Planning on the Edge; Policy Recommendations Addressing Problematic Residential-Industrial District Interfaces

Table 3.6 The Most Problematic Residential-Industrial Interfaces

Group 1 Negative Externality / Group 2 Negative Externality / Negative Externality Produced by Residential District — Community	Air Pollution	Blast Overpressure	Broadcast Interference	Effluent	Fire and Explosive Hazards	Glare	Heat and Humidity	Litter	Lodging Unmerited Complaints	Noise	Odour	On Street Parking	On Street Parking	Outdoor Storage and Waste Material	Particulate Matter	Radiation Emissions	Shortcutting Through Industrial Districts	Toxic and Hazardous Materials	Traffic	Undesirable Social Activity	Unsightly Properties	Vibration	Water Quality Deterioration
Dover					X	X		X		X	X			X				X	X	X	X	X	
Erin Woods					X	X		X		X	X	X	X	X				X	X	X	X	X	
Fairview	X				X	X		X	X	X	X	X	X	X				X	X	X		X	X
Forest Lawn					X	X		X		X	X	X	X	X				X	X	X	X	X	X
Highland Park					X	X		X		X	X	X	X	X				X	X	X		X	
Inglewood	X			X	X	X		X		X	X	X	X	X	X			X	X			X	X
Manchester					X	X				X	X	X	X	X				X	X	X		X	X
Ogden	X			X	X	X	X			X	X	X		X	X	X		X	X			X	X	X
Ramsay	X			X	X	X			X		X	X	X	X	X			X	X			X	X
Vista Heights					X	X				X	X							X					
Winston Hts/Mountview					X	X		X		X	X							X	X		X		

X- denotes presence of condition

3.9 Conclusion

Outputs of industry can adversely effect adjacent residential land uses, and some activities associated with residential land uses can impede performance in industrial districts. The problematic phenomena outlined in the policy of municipalities in Chapter Two were described in greater detail earlier in this chapter. Calgary is home to many large industrial areas, which tend to be located on the eastern side of the city to minimize the effects of westerly wind carried airborne pollutants on populated districts. Even though these industrial areas are newly developed compared with the very old industrial areas of other cities across Canada, there exist areas in Calgary where industry and residences meet to the detriment of one, or both districts. All of the residential communities bordering industrial areas were listed in this chapter and the communities were divided into three categories according to the quality of the interface. The conditions at land use interfaces are never static; new uses and technologies arise to change the nature in which adjacent districts interact. It is the city's responsibility to employ land use policy strategies that keep problematic interfaces from developing in newly developed greenfield areas and remedy land use conflicts at existing interfaces. Many of the land use conflicts occurring in the areas recognized as the most problematic interface areas have continued unabated for generations. Before presenting the recommendations that will attempt to enhance Calgary citywide policy to better address interface conflicts, several ARPs dealing explicitly with residential-industrial interfaces will be reviewed. The ARP review will be accompanied by comments presented by land use planners directly responsible for the creation of the ARPs. The planners were interviewed to discuss how the ARP creation process both succeeded and failed in remedying problematic interface issues. The ideas presented in the next chapter can then be applied to the citywide policy recommendations developed in the concluding chapter of this paper.

Notes

[1] Merriam-Websters, 2002.
[2] Schwab, 1993.
[3] Schawb, 1993.
[4] Schwab, 1993.
[5] Merriam-Websters, 2002.
[6] Farr, 2001.
[7] Schwab, 1993.
[8] Schwab, 1993.
[9] Schwab, 1993.
[10] Edmonton, 1995.
[11] Schwab, 1993.
[12] Schwab, 1993.
[13] Calgary, 2001.

Chapter 4
Interface Policy Created for Calgary Communities

4.1 Introduction

The citywide policies of various municipalities across Canada have been shown to place different degrees of importance on addressing residential-industrial district interface issues. The City of Calgary policies, as shown in Chapter One, do mention the interfaces, however these policies are designed to guide the land management of the city as a whole. In order to understand more fully how the city attempts to remedy problematic interface areas, the Area Redevelopment Plans created for the category 3, most problematic residential-industrial interfaces, will be reviewed in this chapter.

Eleven communities were identified in Chapter Three as being located at Calgary's most problematic industrial interfaces. Community specific policy does not exist for all of these communities, however statutory plans have been created for some of the areas. Several of the communities have undergone the ARP creation process, and others have been the focus of various community studies. Category 3 interface communities selected for review in this chapter were selected based on two factors:

- The presence of an ARP operating within the geographic area
- Access to the chief author of the document

City of Calgary planners were interviewed to determine to what extent the residential-industrial interface was addressed and to rate how the policy interventions succeeded or failed since their adoption by council. This comparison of Calgary ARPs and the input by their authors will complete the analysis of city directed policy for this report. The communities to be addressed in this chapter are listed below.

Forest Lawn	Ogden
Inglewood	Ramsay
Manchester	

The communities listed above represent the older residential areas in Calgary located next to industrial districts. As such, the issues arising in some of these areas have persisted for over 100 years. The industrial interface was but one of the many issues facing the planners in the creation of each ARP. The level of importance placed on dealing with interface issues is specific to each community, however each community ARP contains policy focusing on the interface.

The relevant policy for each category 3 interface community was reviewed. The City of Calgary Planning and Transportation Planning business Unit was approached to identify the principal author of each ARP. The ARP creation process can take several years to complete, and the process represents the synthesis of work conducted by several planners and other city staff. However, there is a senior planner entrusted to oversee the writing of the document and these people were contacted for an interview. The interview guide is located in Appendix O and

Chapter Four- Interface Policy Created for Calgary Communities

interview transcripts are located in appendix P. The five planners approached for interviews were interviewed for no more than 30 minutes and the results of the interviews are described later in the chapter.

There are two category 3 interfaces in Calgary for which no community policy currently exists but there is currently work underway to address the significant residential-industrial interface issues that occur in the areas. The communities of Fairview and Highland Park are located directly adjacent to industrial areas that have existed in Calgary's inner city since the 1950s or earlier. Planners currently involved with developing policy for these areas were interviewed to ascertain how local policy is being drafted to remedy the issues arising at the interfaces.

The ARP interface policies of the five communities are located in the Appendix. A summary of each ARP review and relevant comments from interviewees will be highlighted below. The planners will not be quoted directly; instead, summaries of their comments will be provided.

4.2 What is an Area Redevelopment Plan?

ARPs are statutory plans written to augment the Calgary Plan and provide communities a way in which they can shape the development of their community. The ARP is intended to address issues the Calgary Plan cannot; attention to a much smaller geographic area allows for much greater detail to be placed on community specific issues. The ARPs, as statutory documents, are also meant to be legally binding. This would be the best document available in which to address the problematic residential-interface issues. Each ARP is unique to its specific area and attempts to address the particular issues associated with the adjacent industrial district. According to the Municipal Government Act (MGA), "a council may designate an area of the municipality as a redevelopment area for the purpose of any or all of the following:

1. Preserving or improving land and buildings in the area
2. Rehabilitating buildings in the area
3. Removing buildings from the area
4. Constructing or replacing buildings in the area
5. Establishing, improving or relocating roads, public utilities or other services in the area
6. Facilitating any other development in the area"[1]

The MGA outlines that an ARP can encompass any kind of redevelopment for an area. Once adopted by City Council, ARP policies become statutory policies operating to guide the future development of the area. "The plan must be consistent with any mandatory provincial land use policies and planning regulations in effect and generally should be consistent with any intermunicipal and municipal development plans that affect the area in question."[2]

Traditionally, ARPs are written by city staff in consultation with community groups and other affected parties located within the redevelopment area. "The preparation and adoption of an ARP is also frequently instigated by activist community groups whose objective is to control and minimize the incursion of high density residential and commercial development into the older residential areas in which the members of the group reside."[3] As such, the ARP becomes a preservation tool instead of a redevelopment tool. However, the ARPs have been used, with varied degrees of success, to remedy longstanding issues arising at problematic residential-industrial interfaces.

4.3 ARP Reviews and Interview Results

The industrial interface policies for each of five category 3 interface communities are located in the identified Appendix. A brief introduction to each community and the relevant comments forwarded by each senior planner are included for each of the five category three interfaces.

4.3.1 Forest Lawn-Forest Heights/Hubalta ARP

The Forest Lawn ARP was approved by City Council in September of 1995. Forest Lawn is a community located approximately six kilometres directly east of downtown (see FLN, figure 3.5). The town of Forest Lawn existed as an independent municipality until amalgamation with Calgary in 1961. The town had a population of 13 000 at the time of amalgamation and the area retains many of the characteristics of an independent town, including the presence of a significant industrial area located at the community's eastern margin. This industrial district has been the source of employment and prosperity of first the town and then the community for decades. Alternatively, the problems associated with locating homes directly adjacent to high intensity industry, of which the Hub Oil plant highlighted in Chapter One was an example, are readily apparent in Forest Lawn. The policies pertaining specifically to residential-industrial interfaces are located in Appendix Q.

Jack Scissons was the senior planner responsible for managing the creation of the Forest Lawn ARP. Highlights of information presented during the interview with Jack pertaining to the Forest Lawn ARP are written below. Complete copies of interview summary with Mr. Scissons and the other planners can be found in Appendix P.

Mr. Scissons mentioned that he had worked on the preparation of ARPs for three of the communities recognized in this report as being situated at the most problematic industrial interfaces. Along with Forest Lawn, Mr. Scissons worked on the Ogden and Manchester ARPs, which will be addressed later in this chapter. Mr. Scissons commented that the industrial interface issues were raised in all three of the ARP processes.

The industrial component in the Forest Lawn area, including the heavy industrial operations of Hub Oil and Western Steel, has been a target of complaints launched by adjacent residents for many years. Industry was contacted later in the ARP process and the relationship between residents and industry was, for the most part, confrontational.

Mr. Scissons entered the ARP creation process, in Forest Lawn, Manchester, and Ogden, as the city planner, entrusted by his employer and the community members to find a land use solution through the ARP process. In each case the ARP process was initiated through the standard community directed process, whereby community members perceive a problem or issue, address them to their alderman, who in turn recognizes that significant issues exist in the community to warrant the creation of an ARP.

Mr. Scissons recommended a progressive business/industrial plan to be drawn up for Forest Lawn. This recommendation is described in the ARP as an industrial land use policy calling for the recognition of the area as a mixed use business/industrial park. The plan would involve an intensive tree planting and sign building program. This would serve as an enhancement plan for the area. The 1980 LUB rewrite included retail and commercial uses as well as industrial uses in the I-2 district, but this was later changed through a council amendment because inappropriate commercial uses began to locate in areas not designed to house commercial uses. These areas, including the Forest Lawn industrial area, were characterized by poor quality sidewalks, insufficient lighting, and other commercial insufficiencies emblematic of older industrial areas. However, Mr. Scissons viewed retail and commercial uses in I-2 districts in Forest Lawn as potential catalysts for the survival of older stagnant industrial areas. Council later redesignated much of the Forest Lawn industrial area as a Direct Control district as a result of the ARP policy adoption process. The DC district would employ the same regulations of other I-2 districts with the inclusion of several of the retail uses forbidden from locating in other industrial districts. Commercial uses, according to Mr. Scissons, are a viable alternative for the long-term reinvigoration of this underdeveloped industrial area.

The Business Park concept was not adopted in Forest Lawn due to industry reluctance (the potential for high costs and no immediate gain on investment). In response, Mr. Scissons remains a consummate optimist by stating that there are no planning interventions that have outright failed in Forest Lawn; recommendations just take time to test and implement. For example, both Hub Oil and Western Steel were violators of environmental and other performance standards. Both industries rarely updated their technology, which contributed to their downfall. Hub Oil eventually exploded in a dramatic fire and the site remains developable for I-2 uses, and Western Steel ceased operations instead of dealing with the discovery of high levels of lead poisoning in 15 workers. Contamination has been minimal off-site at Hub Oil and Western Steel because of the low water table and heavy clay content of the soil.

Mr. Scisson's critical recommendation is that "a buffer is required between I-2 and residential space, be it open space or office parks."[4] The key to properly planning for residential-industrial interfaces is determining what buffer strip width is appropriate between residential and industrial land uses. Mr. Scissons proposes a ½ mile wide strip of "clean" industrial uses between heavier industrial uses and residential districts. It will be important to determine which uses are clean and not clean. Providing this buffer, according to Mr. Scissons will save lives and avoid city liability problems.[5]

Summary The Forest Lawn ARP provides specific policies for the improvement of problematic residential-industrial interfaces that have existed in the area for over 50 years. The ARP includes the now commonplace motherhood statements calling for the achievement of compatibility between residential and industrial land uses. The ARP does include sections recommending what specific types of trees can be used as appropriate visual screens and the specific uses that are appropriate to the new direct control industrial area. The most innovative intervention concerning industrial land use in the plan was the attempt at creating a business/industrial park at the community's industrial boundary. Although the conversion of the area into a more visually appealing industrial park has not occurred, the inclusion of expanded commercial and industrial activity has allowed the area to remain economically viable. The ARP includes expansive policy concerning the environmental impacts of the two most problematic industries in the area, Hub Oil and Western Steel. However, this policy was not included in the ARP summary because both operations have ceased operations since the adoption of the ARP, as described earlier in this paper.

Conclusions A field excursion to the Forest Lawn industrial interface reveals a discontinuous and underdeveloped edge. Visually, the industrial area is, for the most part, minimally landscaped and inadequately screened outdoor storage areas abound. The quality of the interface has dramatically improved since the adoption of the Forest Lawn ARP because of the closure of the Hub Oil and Western Steel operations. Both sites sit vacant, awaiting redevelopment. The inclusion of retail and commercial uses in the district may make these areas attractive for commercial style development, but the proximity to truck routes and the rail line make this an attractive location for industry. Land values at the residential side of the interface appear to be low, as the west side of 48 street SE is characterized by rental duplex units. An opportunity exists at interfaces to provide higher quality social or community housing that will remain lower in value because of the presence of industrial neighbours. Eliminating certain industrial uses at interfaces may improve the quality of the interface visually, but it can also act to gentrify the area and remove residents who cannot afford to live elsewhere. This notion, along with the concept of positive externalities produced at interfaces will be expanded in Chapter Five.

4.3.2   Inglewood ARP

Located directly east of the confluence of the Bow and Elbow Rivers, Inglewood is one of Calgary's oldest continuously settled residential areas situated next to industrial operations (see ING, figure 3.5). "Inglewood's isolation has been enforced by some of the noxious impacts of early industries, including the rail yards, stockyards, meat-packers, and later a refinery, a yeast plant, and concrete and steel manufacturers."[6] Earmarked for wholesale redevelopment as an industrial area in the 1960s, the community has succeeded in becoming one of Calgary's most popular communities. Inglewood offers a high quality mix of residential neighbourhoods, many of which are currently being constructed on former industrial sites, a range of entertainment and commercial activities along historic 9th Avenue SE, and the abundance of recreational opportunities located next to the two rivers. As was extensively outlined in Chapter One, Inglewood and Ramsay owe their founding to the location of the rail line through Calgary. Sharing a century long history with Calgary's first industrial district means that the Inglewood and Ramsay ARPs deal extensively with interface issues. The relevant ARP policies are provided in Appendix R.

Philip Dack, City of Calgary Senior Planner, was interviewed to ascertain his attitudes concerning the success of industrial interface policy presented in the Inglewood ARP. The ARP calls for the creation of a cost-sharing programme fund with industries, which has been an underused program. The $10 000 as described in the above policy was made available through the road department for tree planting. The money would be supplied upon redevelopment of industrial properties but this programme has yet to be initiated, according to Mr. Dack. The tree planting programme has city support but the local business and resident initiative is lacking. However, three industrial operations in the area were relocated with monetary incentives supplied by the federal Neighbourhood Improvement Programme (NIP). Moving these operations allowed for interface problems to cease and for residential uses to develop in their stead.

Mr. Dack outlined the particular problems that fuelled resident complaints in Inglewood. Firstly, certain smells from the distillery and yeast plant would reach homes to the east in windy conditions. Secondly, industrial workers often work shift work and they would drive to work at all times of day. These trips would often go through residential streets. Finally, delivery vehicles would uses these roads as 24-hour access points to the businesses. These are all issues that have occurred in Inglewood for many decades.

The conversation turned to the specific issues faced at the former Petro-Canada refinery site. The ARP deals at length with the issues occurring at this large site. Measured levels of contamination dictate that the site cannot be redeveloped for most uses; the city took on management of the site at no financial purchase cost for eventual long-term conversion to a regional park. Houses along the western edge of the refinery were moved to other areas in Ramsay because of the pollution levels. The long-term effect of heavy industry ensures this site, and others, cannot be redeveloped for residential uses.

Successes of the ARP in remedying residential-industrial interfaces include:

- Eliminating industrial uses north of 9th Avenue. Only a remnant of industry remains in this area. The industrial use is limited to the Sears warehouse.

- Mr. Dack referred to this ARP process as a situation where planning actually made a difference. The chief successes were not due to the redesignation of land from industrial to residential uses. Industrially designated sites were located in the area because of restrictive rules precluding other uses from locating in certain areas. As soon as the rules were changed, the land use could be changed to a higher and better use. The key was to identify and then remove certain regulations that were not allowing the area to redevelop according to the opportunities available. Certain regulations were in place that kept redevelopment from occurring on industrial sites, including:

    - Setbacks along 9th Av. The setback rules were relaxed for some development.
    - The Airport Aircraft Noise/Airport Vicinity Protection Area (AVPA) rules were changed. City council was petitioned to allow residential development within the 30-35 Noise Exposure Forecast (NEF) airport sound contour in Inglewood. Council approved, and the provincial cabinet changed the regulation for Inglewood clearing the way for residential redevelopment on formerly industrial land.

- Floodway rules weren't necessarily altered, but the current Inglewood Village site was raised 3 metres to put it above the floodplain. This addition of topsoil also put the site within pollution regulations and made it "non-polluted".

Mr. Dack recognized that redevelopment is risky at pollution sites, but if no pollution is registered, a site should be redeveloped. Sites of pollution can be bought and money placed into a redevelopment fund. This fund could be in the form of a municipal/provincial fund to later clean and redevelop the site, or, the private sector could be encouraged to clean and develop the site with a tax break incentive. Criteria should be developed for the buyout of industrial land, including:

- The presence of a pollution-free site
- The redevelopment of the site should be supported by citywide policy
- A time frame for cleanup and redevelopment should be established
- Tax incentives for a private developer should be provided or a city fund should be established early in the process with a clear goal of redevelopment

Ultimately, Mr. Dack suggests three levels of intervention that will result in possible strategies for the use of older industrial sites:

1. Major Intervention
   - Government buyout and relocation of industrial uses
   - Development of industrial land acquisition criteria
   - Redesignation of industrial land

2. Minor Intervention
   - Development of land use policy tools

3. No Intervention
   - Leave the site and the interface as is

Summary The Inglewood ARP places a high level of importance on remedying long-standing issues at industrial interfaces. The ARP states that industrial uses are inappropriate in the predominantly residential area of the community, and these former industrial sites should be converted to residential use where the results of pollution level testing make this feasible. This has occurred in Inglewood at a furious pace. Former industrial lands are continuing to be redeveloped in the area. It was the identification that certain policy inhibited redevelopment that allowed Mr. Dack to change the appropriate policy and open the area to redevelopment. The industry was removed north of 9th Avenue but the areas remained undeveloped not because of high pollution levels or economic stagnation. On the contrary, the former industrial sites are situated at a prime redevelopment location. Instead, finding unique solutions to side-step existing policy allowed the sites to finally be redeveloped for residential uses. The industrial interface remains in Inglewood south of 9th Av SE and the industry has long been a neighbour of the homes there along the CP rail line. The ARP recognizes this relationship, and instead of calling for the removal of all industry the ARP calls for the development of methods to reduce the impact of adverse effects along the interface. The next chapter of this report will provide such methods.

Conclusions The Inglewood ARP was successful in implementing change for the better concerning residential-industrial interfaces. The ARP called for the elimination of industrial activity north of a specific boundary and for the development of only lighter intensity industry in the remaining industrial areas of the community. The CP line remains and without a plan to redirect the right of way through Calgary, will be a fact of life in the community for the foreseeable future. It is inappropriate to place homes next to rail lines; therefore less intense industrial uses can act to buffer high intensity rail uses from residential areas near rail lines. This strategy was partially employed when the interface between the low-density residential area and the rail line was redesignated as Direct Control in 1993. The industrial sites located between the rail line and the residential area are designated as a DC with I-2 rules prohibiting auto oriented land uses. A buffer zone of sorts is established between homes and heavy industry, however manufacturing uses are still permitted in the DC district. In these older industrial areas, the city must balance the possible adverse impacts of industrial activity on residential areas with the possible impact of removing industry from an area. Chances are these industrial areas are too polluted to support non-industrial uses and too inaccessible to support other commercial or office uses. Traditional industrial uses may be the best land use for this area, but the reduction of the level of intensity of use from heavy industry to light industry was necessary to protect residents from the most problematic hazards located at the industrial interface.

4.3.3 Manchester ARP

The Manchester ARP was adopted by City Council during the production of this paper. This ARP was included because it deals with a unique strategy for redevelopment of an underdeveloped residential community surrounded by industrial land uses. The Manchester community is characterized by a small strip of older single-detached homes surrounded by the industrial uses located in the Central Industrial area to the east and the commercial oriented MacLeod Trail businesses to the west (see MAN, figure 3.5). "Heavy equipment operators, auto body and paint shops, automotive specialty shops, warehouses, offices, and small retail [businesses] predominate this area."[7] Manchester is close to downtown; therefore land values are expected to rise attracting office and commercial uses to the area. The proximity to a LRT station makes this an excellent place to redevelop transit oriented residential land. The policies found in Appendix S outline how the ARP addresses the residential-industrial interface issues that are present and may occur as a result of residential intensification.

Jack Scissons was responsible for the creation of the proposed Manchester ARP. The ARP takes a new approach to redeveloping an older residential area. Most ARP processes involve communities intent on preserving a low-density residential form of their neighbourhood. The Manchester ARP recognizes that the area cannot continue to exist as a low-density residential enclave. The area could have been planned to be entirely commercial, industrial, or office oriented. Instead, Mr. Scissons recognized an opportunity to implement citywide policy by intensifying the density of a vastly underdeveloped inner city residential area. The redevelopment of part of the area to high-density residential use is accompanied by provisions for dealing with potential issues that may arise at the industrial interface.

The Manchester process went much more smoothly than the other ARP processes Mr. Scissons has participated in because all of the affected parties were invited into review sessions at the onset of the process. Also, Manchester is a community with a small population that has been stagnant for many years, and the opposition to residential densification on a large scale is expected to be minimal. The area is ripe for this type of redevelopment and, if the plan is realized, a small, high-density enclave will be sculpted out of the area. The key to the area's long-term success is the minimalization of potential conflicts between the industry and future residents.

Mr. Scissions notes that Manchester was already undergoing a conversion to office use from traditional industrial uses before the Manchester ARP was written due to the area's prime central location. There was potential to create policy converting the entire area to higher density office use. However, the proximity to downtown and the LRT station lead Mr. Scissons to develop the idea to convert the residential areas to a much higher density. Mr. Scissons employed noise studies to show that noise levels above those prescribed in the Calgary Noise Bylaw would not adversely effect the proposed sites of residential redevelopment. Mr. Scissons identifies noise studies as the most effective tool in informing affected parties about the potential for industrially produced nuisances.

Summary The success of the Manchester ARP cannot be gauged because the redevelopment has yet to occur. However, in preparing the ARP, it was recognized that the redeveloped residential areas would be situated next to I-2 designated industrial areas. Commercial uses and green space are to be used as buffers between the two districts. Performance standards levels are to be established as anything detectable by normal sensory perception beyond an industrial building.

Conclusion The underlying assumption of the Manchester ARP is that people will exchange living beside a light industrial area and being potentially affected by the noxious products of industrial activity in exchange for living close to downtown and near the LRT station. If an adverse effect is registered, the ARP calls for that producer of the effect to stop the production of the effect. The policy that "noise, odour, smoke, bright lights or anything of an offensive or objectionable nature"[8] is to be measured by normal sensory perception methods leaves open the potential for subjective analysis of what is a normal sensory perception. What is a foul smell to one person is not to another, who may be a business owner. The Manchester ARP process is a recognition that, in the inner city, a mix of land uses will exist, sometimes in situations where adjacent land uses may impinge on one another. The ARP could benefit from the inclusion of the refined performance standard identification scheme outlined in the next chapter. The potential for risk, especially with the development of high-density residential uses, is not addressed in the ARP, and may be useable in determining which industrial uses may be appropriate to locate adjacent to the new residential developments.

4.3.4 Millican-Ogden Community Revitalization Plan (ARP)

The Ogden ARP is part of a document titled the Millican-Ogden Community Revitalization Plan. The Community Revitalization Plan (CRP) is a more comprehensive type of plan, designed to include the community members in developing their own improvement initiatives and social development plan for the community of Ogden. Ogden is the community located to the west of the Ogden Shops described in Chapter One, and the community has existed as an isolated enclave in Calgary since the construction of the Shops in 1912 (see OGD, figure 3.5). The CRP includes initiatives concerning residential-industrial interfaces but "these initiatives are not approved by council and are accepted for information purposes only."[9] The statutory interface polices will appear in Appendix T while the non-statutory policies can be found in Appendix U.

A raised berm and the CP rail line separate the residential areas of Ogden from the Ogden Shops to the east. A vacant former oil refinery site lies to the north of the residential area. The residential area adjacent to the refinery site, known as Lynnview Ridge, has been the focus of community concern since environmental test results showed the area contains unsafe levels of contaminants.[=] The South Hill area, directly adjacent to heavy industry, defines the south margin of Ogden. There is little mention of the Ogden Shops interface in the ARP, but the South Hill area warrants extensive mention. The South Hill residential area is comprised of assorted single family dwellings and two trailer parks, the South Hill and Caravan Mobile Home Parks, located south of Glenmore Trail. In past policy, the city has indicated the intention of replacing the existing residential area with light industrial uses. The Ogden ARP reverses this trend and calls for the long-term preservation of residential land use in the area

Themes prevailing in the Manchester ARP resonate in the Ogden ARP. The City of Calgary has used a virtually identical live-work policy in both of the plans. There is an understanding that industrial activity should have the ability to continue operations next to residential areas. This does support Calgary Plan policy. In the interview, Mr. Scissons mentioned how the Ogden ARP process was fundamentally different from all other previous and subsequent ARP exercises. Although initiated by the city, the community residents had a greater stake in the completion of policy and shaped the formation of much of the Community Plan section. Even though the ARP includes the input of a vast array of people, the City need not adhere to the policy guidelines expressed in the non-statutory part of the ARP.

The Ogden Shops industrial interface was not mentioned to a significant degree in the ARP because Mr. Scissons stated the ARP committee had little control or ability to influence the business side of the study area. Because the CPR and other high intensity businesses were located outside the council defined study area, the specifics of the businesses could not be addressed in the plan. However, because all players were invited early to the process and some of the problems associated with the interface were included inside the study area, the plan was successful in addressing some issues at the problematic interface, especially in the South Hill area. The industries and the residents in this part of Ogden could learn about each other through establishing a dialogue. Bringing both sides of the disputed area to the table at the onset of the process allowed for a viable solution to be proposed.

[=] The levels of measured contaminants have not increased in the area, but, in 1999, the regulations governing safe levels of contamination were changed. The area became unsafe only because the safety levels were changed, not because the absolute level of pollution increased.

Again, Mr. Scissons comments that the most successful solution in looking at residential-industrial interfaces is conducting noise studies. The noise studies not only satisfied the Approving Authority mandate, in this case, the Calgary Planning Commission, but also provided the evidence that the residential uses on South Hill could coexist with adjacent industry, under certain conditions such as providing noise walls. The noise study is not used in this instance to prove industry is producing an unacceptable level of noise. On the contrary, the noise study results were used to show the noise produced by the industry was acceptable and the interface issues were negligible, allowing the trailer parks to remain. The South Hill Mobile Home Park has evolved into a mobile home park of the highest quality, complete with landscaped parks, a pathway system, paved roads, and connections to all major city services. The community used the noise study to prove it can coexist with the industry and that the mobile home neighbourhood should not be relocated.

Mr. Scissons introduces the live-work concept in the Ogden document. This live-work development area is to locate at the border with the Ogden Shops. At the time of writing this report, the live-work concept has yet to become a viable alternative for the people of Ogden, although it was anticipated that it may take several years for the live-work option to become popular.

Mr. Scissons reports that problems also arose with smells emanating from adjacent offensive neighbour industries (including from the Alberta Processing Plant, which manufactured animal feed from animal carcasses). The strong smells emanating from the plant became a great matter of concern for the community members as members of the community discussed the operation of the plant with family members. It so turned out that the industrial neighbours, including the Alberta Processing Plant, employed a significant portion of the community and funded many community enterprises. Even as some industrial operations produced the negative externalities found in the community, they simultaneously employed a large number of community members and backed local initiatives. Ogden acts as a microcosm for any city with an industrial economic base. As much as industrial activity can be a nuisance and potentially harmful, the same activity fuels the municipal economy.

Summary Intensive industrial operations have flanked the eastern side of the Ogden community since its inception. The community owes its existence to the location of the neighbouring Ogden Shops. There has always been an understanding in Ogden that certain side effects of industrial activity are to be dealt with. The ARP recognizes this in policy designed to allow existing residential-industrial interfaces to remain. The difficulty comes in deciding what levels of nuisance are acceptable. The city prescribed levels for noise were used to prove the mobile home parks on the South Hill could coexist, but intermittent sound and smell are difficult to monitor, especially with a subjective tool like human sensory perception.

Conclusion The Lynnwood Ridge remediation process continues in Ogden. The former owners of the former refinery, the City of Calgary, the provincial government and area residents are deciding how to compensate residents who now feel their homes and property are valueless, and that they have suffered harm because of the high level of contaminants in the ground. Even when an industrial operation controls the production of negative externalities over the course of its business life, there is always the possibility that the unmeasured long term effects of operation will affect adjacent residential areas. Affordable housing developments often choose to locate at more marginalized interfaces, of which Lynnview Ridge is an example. The appropriateness of placing any new residential uses next to industry with the potential to contaminate surrounding land should be addressed by the City and discussed with residents.

4.3.5 Ramsay ARP

The final ARP examined in this report is the Ramsay ARP approved in 1994. Tim Creelman was the City of Calgary Senior Planner who spearheaded the ARP creation process. Ramsay has experienced many of the same issues as Inglewood, however Ramsay has yet to undergo the same intensive redevelopment that has occurred in Inglewood. Both communities exist because of the orientation of the railway, and industry has existed along with residential uses since the community's origins (see RAM, figure 3.5). Industrial land use designations comprised one-third of the land area of the community at the time the ARP was written. Over half of that industrial land was vacant. Refer to Appendix V for specific ARP policies.

In the interview, Mr. Creelman stated that the interface issues in Ramsay were revealed in the ARP creation process. Other issues, including concerns associated with the proximity of the Stampede Grounds were of greater importance at the onset of the process. However, the interface issues grew in importance as the process unfolded. More important than the quality of the interface itself were traffic issues associated with the industrial areas located to the south and east of the residential area and the use and propagation of signage.

The industrial interface issue received a great deal of attention in the ARP because the Dominion Bridge industrial operation took a vested interest in dealing with the community. An employee of Dominion Bridge was a member of the Community Planning Committee. The plan succeeded at having some land between the community and Stampede zoned as park space (PE), from its former Agricultural use (A). Although not a residential-industrial buffer, the use of land redesignation to create a buffer could be used in a residential-industrial setting. According to Mr. Creelman, a great success of the plan was the removal of all I-3 land use designations from the plan boundaries, and the insertion of lower intensity I-2 uses into these areas.

Summary Like the Inglewood ARP, the Ramsay ARP identifies the problematic interface areas and prescribes policies for allowing the residential and commercial uses to coexist. The use of development guidelines outlines specific recommendations that are to be enacted, including the shadowing and perimeter area depth limits. The worst problems that may continue along interfaces are to be phased out of the area with the redesignation of I-3 heavy industrial land use to light industrial uses along the interface. The need for a major development proposal for large portions of the vacant industrial lands to provide a concept and site plan specifically addressing the interface with adjacent residential areas is reminiscent of the Industrial Statutory Plans used in Edmonton. Where new industrial redevelopments border residential areas, the developer is required to prepare a plan detailing how the adjacent residential area will be affected. This provision for a plan may be appropriate for inclusion in citywide policy.

Conclusions Nearly ten years after the ARP was adopted in Ramsay, redevelopment activity in the community continues but not at the scale experienced in other inner city communities, including Inglewood. The redesignation of land at the industrial interface has not changed the fact that the effects of industrial activity are still felt by adjacent residents. The higher intensity industrial uses are still operational in the redesignated areas as non-conforming uses. The redesignation of land use to less intense use will eventually alter the conditions of the interface, but the long-term nature of the solution is insufficient in removing inappropriate uses from the interface.

4.4 Ongoing Problematic Interface Study Areas

There exist other category 3 interface communities beyond the five mentioned above that have recently been the focus of study by the city of Calgary. Significant work has been conducted in these areas in the interest of remedying the problematic interfaces but the areas in question have not been addressed in an area specific ARP. As the political climate changes and ways of addressing specific planning issues evolve, the likelihood that ARPs will be created in the manner in which they have been produced in the past two decades is declining. The City of Calgary is exploring new statutory policy initiatives that are issue specific and use fewer resources to produce. The communities of Highland Park and Fairview have experienced problems associated with being located next to industrial neighbours for many years. The results of interviews with two planers who worked extensively in each area will be presented to assess the status of residential-industrial policy creation in these areas. The move to new types of community planning and the revision of the Calgary LUB offer an unprecedented opportunity to enact citywide policy in these areas that may have a measurable effect on improving the quality of the problematic interface.

4.4.1 Fairview

Located in south central Calgary adjacent to the southern margin of the Central Industrial area (see FAI, figure 3.5), Fairview is located at one of the most contentious residential-industrial interfaces in Calgary. To the south of the interface is located a single-detached residential area, and to the north of the interface is located a light industrial district designated as I-2. The two districts are separated by a back alley. The residential side of the interface was built out by 1962 and the industrial sites were developed by 1976. However, both land use districts were approved by City Council at the same time in the 1950s. The provisions on the current Calgary LUB "include industrial performance standards that provide regulations intended to protect communities from hazards and to protect industries from arbitrary exclusion based solely on nuisance production."[10] The application of performance standards has been insufficient in resolving land use conflicts as affected residents have been raising formal concerns with the city of Calgary since the 1970s. "For example, in 1979, the residents petitioned the City to address vibration and noise levels generated by an illegally operating business."[11] The problems continued until 1989, when the Operations and Development Committee of the City recommended that a "buffer or sound attenuation structure be constructed in the alley."[12] The cost for the structure was to be shared between the city, the residents, and industrial landowners, but it was never built.

"Ongoing resident concerns regarding traffic, parking, noise, pollution, property damage and unsightly industrial premises continue in Fairview."[13] A mediation process initiated in 1998 requiring voluntary co-operation between residents and industrial operators accomplished little in the area. A November 2001 fire on an industrial site caused the release of chemicals from the site and the evacuation of residents and employees within a one-kilometre radius of the site. "The fire has heightened resident concerns regarding the storage and use of potentially hazardous chemicals on industrial lands."[14] The Calgary Fire Department is currently undertaking a study concerning the storage of hazardous material. The Fairview situation highlights how a known and well-documented problematic interface has not been adequately addressed for over 20 years. Diane Hooper, a planner who has worked extensively on the Fairview interface project, was interviewed for her thoughts concerning the process.

Ms. Hooper's initial strategy was to go through a land use redesignation process on the industrial side of the interface. Responsibility for the Fairview project was given to her in 2000, at the completion of the mediation process. At the end of the mediation process, it was clear there was no opportunity to solve the issues between residents and industry through mediation. The mediation committee was abolished and a Land Use Committee was created in its stead. Through working with the Land Use Committee, Ms. Hooper suggested that land in the industrial area be redesignated to limit the scope of industrial uses allowed in the interface area. The new use zone would not be a DC zone, but would be a new industrial interface zone that could be used in other interface areas in the City. The new land use area would act to eventually phase out existing noxious uses as they were sold or moved from the area through the adoption of strict performance controls. Immediate shorter term solutions included the placing of fencing or soft landscaping (hedges and trees) along the interface and augmenting operational traffic solutions, including barring loading and unloading in the alley.

The Mediation Committee and then Land Use Committee process succeeded in bringing people to the bargaining table. Additional success has been difficult to achieve in this process because the issues along the Fairview interface have existed for so long that the animosity between industrial owners and residents is pervasive. According to Ms. Hooper, industrial business owners have not been motivated to find a solution as they have not been adversely affected by residential neighbours. The business owners have been reluctant to limit the scope of industrial uses as recommended by the Land Use Committee.

Summary According to Ms. Hooper, the planner cannot neglect the influence of politics in a land use policy decision. The decision to adopt a policy ultimately rests with politicians who, for a variety of reasons, may or may not act to provide a solution to long standing planning issues. What the people of Fairview have been left with is a problematic land use issue that has been without an effective planning solution since the development of the interface in the 1960s.

Conclusions The Fairview process has been riddled with indecision and inaction. A generation has elapsed since the noise, odour, traffic, and other problems were first reported in Fairview. Fairview is not the same type of community as Ogden or Forest Lawn. The housing types found at the interface are mostly well maintained owner occupied single family homes. The people who live in these homes may have received a bargain when they bought the home but they desire the protection from noxious products of industrial activity experienced by other homeowners in the City. Industrial activity has been intended for the north part of the alley since Fairview's initial subdivision. The businesses located there have thrived due to their central location. Homeowners in Fairview have had the opportunity since the day they bought their property to check on the intended land use of the area north of their homes; industrial businesses should not be expected to move out of the area instantly. A solution must be implemented soon in Fairview. If the redesignation solution had been initiated twenty years ago, the nature of the industrial area may have already changed according to market forces and the interface would likely have already improved with the removal of the most offensive industrial uses.

4.4.2   Highland Park

The Highland Park community is located in North Central Calgary and it borders the Greenview industrial area, part of the Northeast Industrial area, to the east (see HPK, figure 3.3). Jim Francisco prepared a non-statutory Industrial Business Plan for the Highland industrial area in 1998. The plan provides strategies "that will help stimulate redevelopment and re-investment in the area"[15], and in so doing identifies interface issues in the area. The Highland Park residential-industrial interface shares many similarities with the Fairview interface. The two areas are approximately equidistant to downtown, close to truck transportation routes, have a long history of conflict between the incompatible land uses, and share a significant interface along a back alley. Highland Park is included in the North Bow Design Brief, a statutory plan covering a large portion of northern Calgary adopted in 1977.[≡] A striking difference between Highland Park and Fairview is the condition of the interface. The industrial and residential sides of the interface are comprised of poorer maintained structures than those found in Fairview. The Highland Park interface is likely addressed to a lesser extent than the Fairview interface not because significantly problematic issues do not occur in Highland Park. Highland Park may have attracted less attention from planners because area residents are less likely to voice concerns about the problems associated with industrial activity in exchange for lower housing costs.

Mr. Francisco first mentioned how the Design Brief contains policy concerning a tree-planting program to be conducted in the area. The trees were never planted along 1st Av NE. The interface at 1st Av NE is still in a decaying condition because the local residential property owners were unwilling to provide resources for the Local Improvement By-Law. Mr. Francisco's ideas for providing a quick fix for the area were:

- Planting trees as a screen, which was subsequently not approved by parks because of the low probability of tree survival.
- Screening by placing plastic strips in chain link fences.

A committee was formed in the area in 1998 to work on the creation of the Industrial Business Plan and the results of the work of this committee were the improvements done to roads in the interior of the industrial area. Parking problems remained of paramount importance. Cars are parked all over the area, including illegally on boulevards and setbacks which tends to

---

[≡] Design Briefs predate Area Redevelopment Plans as area specific statutory plans and are of the same basic format and intent.

damage the landscaping around the businesses. However, getting repairs done to the interior roads seemed sufficient to the business owners, according to Mr. Francisco.

A possible long-term solution was the idea generated by Mr. Francisco to create an Industrial Business Revitalization Zone. Because the Greenview area is a significant employment area (approximately 3000 employed), the BRZ would improve the leveraging power of the local businesses. The alderman at the time of producing the Industrial Business Plan was interested in creating a business association of some kind in the area to mobilize the local interests. The business association would act to co-ordinate simple improvement measures, including tree planting, screening, and parking. However, the individualist nature of the independent businessmen made this difficult. The local businessmen continue to squabble about many issues, including parking. Also, there is reluctance to create a BRZ, or even quasi-BRZ organization because of the perception of what BRZs create, which seems inappropriate for industry (street furniture, sidewalk improvements, banners, etc.).

Mr. Francisco sees a need in Calgary for a new industrial designation different from the existing I-2 land use designation that would provide for less intensive and smaller scale industrial uses that do not require high levels of planning intervention (expansive setbacks, soft landscaping, etc.). This new land use district would be designed for smaller parcel industrial uses. Another possible land use solution is the implementation of a blanket Direct Control policy that would apply to the entire area. The DC could address the urban design guidelines, setbacks, landscaping, and parking. A rethinking of the land use in the area, including the list of permitted and discretionary uses, is required because small lot industrial sites are being lost to non-industrial uses, for example a former drive-in site is being redeveloped as a church site.

Mr. Francisco identified the major interface problems as:

- parking along residential streets (1st Av NE)
- many industrial businesses have struck parking agreements with City agencies that make it difficult to control parking through by-law regulations or to maintain parking standards across the area
- noise
- light pollution
- traffic$^\Theta$
- other pollution (fumes, liquids, etc.)

The area as a whole tends to be filled with a wide range of low intensity industrial uses that are dependent upon customers living in the surrounding area. The area also functions as a local industrial service area. As such, the existing industrial area serves an important local commercial service function whose continued presence, according to Calgary Plan policy, should be encouraged as long as the residential and industrial neighbours can coexist.

Summary Mr. Francisco's work in the residential-industrial interface area came from the perspective of the local businessman. What seemed to be important to the local businessmen

---

$^\Theta$ However, improving road conditions along 1st St NE may make it a more popular truck route creating even more traffic associated problems.

was the ability to carry out business unimpeded. Participants never adopted the BRZ programme for Highland Park and the fence building programme for Fairview because of the reluctance, of both residents and businesspeople to incur costs to improve the area. As seen in Chapter Three, there are fewer ways in which residential districts can negatively affect industrial areas, and business owners will likely continue to engage in industrial activities that produce a negative externality unless that activity is controlled by an agency with the power to halt the activity or penalize the producer.

Conclusions Industry cannot be removed at the residential-industrial interface without reason. Calgary policy recognizes that industry is needed in the city, and it is sometimes located next to inappropriate neighbours. In some situations, this relationship must be improved or the interface condition will have to change. Approaching businessmen and residents to enter into a voluntary remediation process may only be a tactic used by industry to placate affected residents. Sometimes, certain regulations must be adopted that are detrimental to an affected interest group for the betterment of the entire community. If a group of businesses in an industrial area has been afforded every opportunity to improve a problematic interface but they have not limited the production of negative externalities, then the interface may have to be improved by other means, which we will included in the concluding chapter.

4.5 ARP Industrial Interface Policy Comparison

The five ARPs examined in this chapter address the issues associated with problematic interfaces in different ways. The following table will highlight the overall industrial policies of each ARP, the specific interface policies, and the failures and successes of each ARP as described by the interviewed planner.

Figure 4.1- ARP Policy Review and Comments of Senior Planners

ARP & Planner	Overall Industrial Policies	Specific Interface Policies	Shortcomings of the ARP	Successes of the ARP
Forest Lawn- Jack Scissons	-more retail and commercial uses are permitted in I-2 -48 St identified as specific interface -interface tree planting programme proposed	-detailed treatment of specific industrial sites (i.e. Hub Oil) -specific tree species mentioned for interface	-48 St remains as a harsh edge with limited interface treatment (few trees) -Policy was not the impetus for the departure of Hub Oil and Western Steel	-inclusion of retail uses has kept the area economically viable
Inglewood- Philip Dack	-cost sharing tree planting programme proposed -industry to be removed north of 9 Av -heavy industry to be removed from community	-detailed treatment of specific industrial sites (i.e. Russell Steel) -clean-up of polluted sites proposed -financial program for screening proposed	-no significant tee planting a the interface has occurred -clean-up at some industrial sites (Petro-Canada refinery) is difficult due to high contamination levels	-most industry north of 9 Av was relocated -intense residential redevelopment of old industrial land north of 9 Av
Manchester- Jack Scissons	-the light industrial component adjacent to the CP rail line are slated to remain	-commercial & live-work uses to buffer industrial & residential sites	-as yet unknown (policy adopted in 2002) -possibility of nuisance complaints	-may produce the vibrant inner city enclave envisioned in the ARP

Chapter Four- Interface Policy Created for Calgary Communities

Millican-Ogden Jack Scissons	-existing South Hill areas to remain residential	-live-work sites proposed	-presence of Ogden Shops not adequately addressed	-South Hill trailer parks and industry coexistence
Ramsay- Tim Creelman	-heavy industrial uses in community to be changed to light industrial -industrial traffic mentioned -concept plan required for major redevelopment	-specific Development Guidelines established for each of the three subareas of the interface	-the redevelopment of industrial operations along the interface has been a slow process -heavy uses remain in interface districts	-heavy industrial uses have been removed from interface

4.6 Conclusion

Area Redevelopment Plans have been effective in addressing concerns at residential-industrial interfaces and have acted to improve conditions at many of Calgary's more problematic areas. The ARP is increasingly not being used by the City of Calgary to address issue driven planning processes in communities. The ARPs, even though they are statutory documents, can be misinterpreted or ignored by planners, other city staff, and politicians. The amount of time it takes to create a traditional ARP can be so long that the adopted document is no longer relevant to the community concerns. The ARP process is usually community (resident) driven and ignores the needs of adjacent businesses. The ARP process, as it has been institutionalized, has come to be seen as an obsolete process providing Band-Aid solutions. The City of Calgary is attempting to create community planning initiatives that identify planning problems at their onset, before the planner has to play catch up and prescribe reactive policy. Community issues are increasingly perceived as occurring at a regional scale, and the scale of recent planning projects reflects this change. Increasingly, planning exercises are increasing the geographic scope of the study areas. No matter how the planning processes are changed to be more responsive or pro-active to community needs, the success of planning will be rated on how well the policy is followed through. The review of community statutory policy and planner feedback about the relative success of the policy will now be added to the findings of the previous three chapters to present the options for Calgary outlined in Chapter Five.

Notes

[1] Alberta, 2000.
[2] Laux, 1997.
[3] Laux, 1997.
[4] Scissons, 2002.
[5] Scissons, 2002.
[6] Calgary, 1993.
[7] Calgary, 2002.
[8] Calgary, 2002.
[9] Calgary, 1999.
[10] Calgary, 2002.
[11] Calgary, 2002.
[12] Calgary, 2002.
[13] Calgary, 2002.
[14] Calgary, 2002.
[15] Calgary, 1998.

Chapter 5
Options for Calgary Interfaces

5.1 Introduction

Residential and industrial districts will continue to be located adjacent to one another and situations will continue to arise where the products of residential or industrial activity will negatively effect the neighbour. The potential exists to employ strategies to improve the quality of life for both residential and industrial uses at the interface. This paper does not mark the first attempt at addressing the residential-industrial interface issue specifically. In 1990, Calgary City Council established the Task Force on Industrial and Commercial Sites. The task force was established to investigate the impact of active and former industrial sites on residential communities. The task force was unable to develop policy for enhancing land use management of the interfaces."

This chapter will first explore the range of options that may be applicable to Calgary. These options were developed through the work completed in the previous four chapters; in no way is the list of options exhaustive but it does represent a wide range of policy options available to be employed by municipalities. The options most appropriate to the Calgary situation according to the interviewed planners and the researcher will then be compared to rate their appropriateness in improving interface areas in Calgary.

5.2 The Range of Options

The options available for improving problematic interfaces range from continuing to employ existing policy to fundamentally altering the ways in which land use designation is conducted. The following descriptions of the options will be divided into two groups. The first set of options will be related to the Land Use Bylaw. These options, 5.2.1-5.2.5, require continued interpretation or a possible change to the LUB. The second set of options, 5.2.6-5.2.8, provides policy regulations not directly addressed within the LUB. These options could be applied to problematic interfaces without any reworking of the LUB. Within either group of options the less intrusive changes will be presented first, proceeded by more interventionist policy alterations. Many of these options are not mutually exclusive and can be used in combination with other options to best suit the planning situation. The appropriateness of the options to the Calgary context will be summarized at the conclusion of the chapter.

" The majority of sites investigated by the Task Force on Industrial and Commercial Sites (1991) "were located in the southeast quadrant [of Calgary], which encompasses most of the city's heavy industrial districts as well as older communities such as Inglewood, Ramsay, Ogden and Forest Lawn, which contain a mixture of industrial and residential uses. Residents of these communities complain frequently to their Alderman about the noise, dust, odours, traffic and/or unsightly appearance of nearby activities." The task force conducted preliminary research work but the recommendations to help reduce impacts were never implemented.

5.2.1 Continued Use of Existing Policy

Purpose- Land uses are segregated into different districts with imposed site and building (development) standards in order to minimize nuisance.[1]

Perhaps the most readily accepted option for managing problematic interfaces would be continuing to deal with the interfaces through the currently used policy framework. The existing interface policies of the Calgary Plan and the Land Use Bylaw would remain in place and the use of other policy strategies, including ARPs, would continue. The Inglewood and Ramsay ARPs highlighted in Chapter Four have been successful at alleviating some of the long-term problems that have occurred at interfaces. The removal of pocket industrial sites in residential districts and the redesignation of adjacent industrial land from heavy to light industrial has vastly improved Inglewood and Ramsay. The political reality of Calgary dictates that ARPs will likely not be written for the remaining most problematic interface areas or that existing ARPs will be reviewed in a timely fashion.

The City could also continue to employ Direct Control designations to create site specific policy designed to improve interface areas. This strategy was used in Ramsay and Inglewood along the industrial interface to limit some of the industrial uses that could potentially locate there. This strategy is effective for areas that require a rapid change in land use policy. The Fairview Land Use studies identifies this as a viable option for the industrial area abutting the residential community. The industrial sites adjacent to homes could be redesignated as a DC area with essentially the same rules of the I-2 district in place; the uses that create the adverse effects for the community could be removed from the permitted use list. These businesses would become categorized as legal non-conforming land uses. The business could continue to operate in perpetuity, but if the business chose to expand or change the nature of operation, it would have to relocate because the use would become non-conforming. The City has the authority, under the Municipal Government Act (MGA), to redesignate privately owned sites if the redesignation is deemed to serve the public interest. Redesignating sites of potential health hazards located across a lane from a residential neighbourhood would likely qualify as serving the public good.

The use of Direct Control districts to manage problematic interfaces provides a long-term solution for the most problematic areas. It could take several years for businesses to be encouraged to relocate from an area. It would prove more difficult to encourage movement of businesses in a less active marketplace with stalled property values. The Direct Control redesignation option might be politically hazardous to implement for politicians interested in preserving the economic viability, and voter confidence, of industrial operators along with the health of adjacent residents. As described in Chapter One, the use of DC districts is troublesome because of other administrative reasons. Effective land use policies encapsulated in DC districts may go unseen by other planners and developers because of the proliferation of DC district use. These districts that encourage truly innovative land uses, like the work-live development located at a residential-industrial interface in Ramsay, can go unheralded because of the sheer number of DC districts in existence. The potential to formulate new industrial districts instead of additional interface DC districts will be described in a subsequent section.

5.2.2 New Style Community Planning

Purpose- The purpose remains the same as for the previous section but special studies are employed instead of ARPs to tackle issues specific to a particular geographical area that may or may not share boundaries with a traditional community planning area.

ARPs are no longer the most popular method of addressing community scale planning issues. Special studies and other statutory policies are being used more to address issue specific concerns. A residential-industrial interface special study would provide guiding policy for an interface area that stretches along several communities. This continuous linear interface is found along the edges of Forest Lawn, Erin Woods, and Dover. Applying community plans to larger geographic areas provides policy much more detailed than citywide policy and limits the redundancy of providing virtually identical policy for each individual community. Creating policy for a specific issue will limit the amount of ancillary material in the document, help to streamline the public participation process, and achieve a policy direction before the process becomes irrelevant. Interface policy could be applied to multiple communities affected by similar interface issues. This would be applicable to Calgary as many communities sharing a common industrial boundary experience similar negative externalities.

5.2.3 Performance Based Industrial Land Use Planning

Purpose- "The central concept behind industrial performance standards is that, so long as industrial enterprises can operate in a fashion that avoids the creation of various enumerated nuisances, they should be free to locate anywhere within an industrial zone."[2]

Pure performance based industrial zoning would not prescribe certain uses for certain districts. The performance based system would be used to determine separation distances between land use districts. Quantifiable conditions of industrial activity, like glare, noise, odour, air pollution and others listed in Chapter Three, would be measured against standards included in the land use policy to determine if the use was appropriate to the site. The performance levels may be standard for each site boundary. For example, if a land use policy for a city states that a business cannot produce noise levels above 60 decibels beyond the site boundary, then any use forecasted to produce noise over that level at the boundary would not be able to locate there or would have to change the scale of the operation. This would "allow even the 'dirtiest' industries to demonstrate their creativity in redesigning their operations to meet the standards."[3] The performance standard would effectively create a buffer transition zone.

The City of Calgary and the majority of municipalities mentioned in Chapter Two employ some form of performance based zoning. Performance based zoning could apply to all land use districts but most municipalities apply performance standards to the measurable by-products of industrial activity. Many municipalities across North America have switched from the land use zoning approach of listing permitted and discretionary uses to performance based zoning for industrial land. "These lists of industry by category, based on the industries' historical characteristics, often become outdated. They fail to recognize both the changes that occur as industry evolves and the degree of flexibility that often exists in industry operations."[4] It is the nature of industry to change and adapt quickly, therefore a rigid industrial land use bylaw cannot adequately address new industrial uses that develop quickly. For example, the 1980 Calgary LUB was incapable of anticipating the growth of telecommunication and information technology industries that has occurred in the past 20 years. From an economic development perspective, being unable to quickly accommodate new industry because of inflexible land use regulations can damage a city's potential for growth. The LUB has been amended to include new uses, but the strength of the performance based approach would be to allow any use and then gauge the appropriateness of the development based on effects on neighbouring districts. The effects of industrial activity would be quantifiable and measured against standardized norms using standardized equipment.

A pure performance based zoning system is difficult to implement because all possible externalities, many of which are outlined in Chapter Three, cannot be measured and accounted for completely. The performance based system requires that every development application be measured according to the possible performance based impacts. Approving uses based on permitted or discretionary criteria affords a level of understanding between applicant and approving authority that is absent in performance based zoning. Measuring or forecasting the effects of industrial activity for every development can be time consuming and unnecessary.

Performance based zoning can be used effectively in concert with land use designations dividing certain uses into zones if the conditions to be controlled by performance criteria are properly defined and listed. The performance code should also include information as to which level of government is responsible for which particular negative externality. "Municipalities should reach clear agreement with extra jurisdictional authorities on the boundaries of enforcement and regulatory responsibility."[5] Displaying this information in a table directly within the LUB will avoid confusion when determining which effects of problematic industrial activity at interfaces are to be monitored and policed by which levels of government. A sample of this chart will be developed for the Policy Recommendations for Calgary section to follow.

5.2.4   Risk Based Land Use Planning

Purpose- **Risk based land use planning is intended to "regulate the location of industrial uses (specifically those that use or produce hazardous substances) with the objective of minimizing, to some acceptable level, the potential impacts that an emergency or accident could occur, in terms of casualties or property damage."[6]**

The idea of planning according to Risk Management originated in Europe. The LUB would classify hazardous activities and delineate which activities could locate around certain hazards. A risk assessment is a required part of the development application process for any prospective development that may involve a hazardous use or other developments attempting to locate near a hazardous use. Therefore, industries with the potential to produce negative externalities would need to produce a risk assessment to address the possible impact on adjacent areas. Conversely, a residential development applicant would have to produce a risk assessment

94

if the development were to locate close to a externality producing industrial operation. Risk based planning is designed to protect industries from incursion by other land uses as well as adjacent land uses for the adverse effects of industry.

Situations exist whereby businesses will produce some form of negative externality. The Major Industrial Accidents Council of Canada (MIACC) guidelines recognize that the safety of citizens must be of paramount concern. "Decisions regarding land use for businesses have often been based on the greater public interest, recognizing that there might be local social and environmental tradeoffs; however, public safety cannot be compromised in such tradeoffs and an acceptable level of safety must be assured."[7] Certain nuisance adverse effects, including those experienced at Category 2: Nuisance Only Residential-Industrial Interfaces can be managed by performance standard techniques. MIACC states that safety must not be compromised at certain hazardous interfaces.

MIACC guidelines were established based on risk levels first developed for the Netherlands. The Netherlands government established that "the maximum acceptable level for new major hazard installations for individual risk has been taken as the risk level which increases the risk of death by all other causes with a maximum of one percent. The individual 'natural death' risk run by the population group of 10 to 14 year olds, which is 1 in 10 000 per year, has been taken as the basic risk."[8] The maximum allowable risk is therefore 1% of 10 000, or 1 in 1 000 000. "In other words, the risk of a fatal accident to which an individual is exposed because of his continued presence (365 days per year) in the neighbourhood of a hazardous activity shall be less than one in a million years."[9]

MIACC has established the following guidelines for land uses that can locate in risk contours according to the acceptable levels of risk. It is important to note that these guidelines do not prohibit all activities or structures within the various risk contours, but rather restrict land use within each zone.[10] Figure 5.1 shows these risk contours applied to a typical urban area.

Figure 5.1- MIACC Guidelines for Acceptable Levels of Risk (Source- MIACC, 1997)

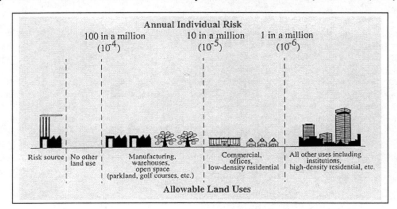

- **"From risk source to 1 in 10 000 risk contour:**
  - No other land uses except the source facility, pipeline, or corridor
- **1 in 10 000 to 1 in 100 000 risk contours:**
  - uses involving continuous access and the presence of limited numbers of people but easy evacuation, e.g. open space (parks, golf courses, conservation areas, trails, excluding recreation facilities such as arenas), warehouses, manufacturing plants
- **1 in 100 000 to 1 in 1 000 000 risk contours:**
  - uses involving continuous access but easy evacuation, e.g., commercial uses, low-density residential areas, offices
- **Beyond the 1 in 1 000 000 risk contour:**
  - All other land uses without restriction including institutional uses, high-density residential areas, etc."[11]

The City of Edmonton has adopted a risk assessment based approach to industrial land use zoning, the specifics of which are outlined in Chapter Two. This system is appropriate to Edmonton because of the presence of large-scale oil refinery operations located on the east side of that city, and in the adjacent Refinery Row area of Strathcona County. Strathcona County was not included in the comparison analysis in Chapter 2 because it did not meet the selection criteria for this paper. However, it is important to mention that Strathcona County was able to create transition zones similar to the MIACC guidelines between the heavy industry oil operations and other uses because much of the land located adjacent to the refineries at the time of implementation of the transition zones was undeveloped. The situation is much different for Edmonton, as significant residential development existed within MIACC prescribed risk contours before the transition zones were developed. The City of Edmonton decided it was not feasible to relocate the homes in neighbouring communities or to create the transition zones and make all of the homes within the zone nonconforming uses. Edmonton employs a hybrid risk MIACC risk management approach that is effective because of an open and effective line of communication between adjacent heavy industrial oil operations and the adjacent residents.

Difficulties with the risk based system of land use management are similar to those for performance based approaches. Like performance standard forecasts, risk assessments completed for every development locating near an industrial operation could be time consuming and costly. This is a procedural issue that would be improved as the administration and developers learned how to interpret and create risk assessment reports. However, at the core of risk based planning is the notion that "land-use planning should consist of two elements: general zoning for hazardous industrial activities, taking into account all aspects of protecting health and the environment, including property; and case-by-case decision-making concerning the siting of a new installation or proposed development near an existing installation."[12] In a municipality characterized by heavy industrial uses known to use or store hazardous material, risk based planning may be the option most appropriate to ensure the safety of the citizenry.

5.2.5 Land Use Bylaw Rewrite

The Calgary LUB is currently under review. A number of possibilities exist in deciding how residential-industrial interfaces are to be addressed. The policy options included in this paper could be added to the existing industrial land use districts in the rewrite process. The introduction of the industrial section would include a more definite list of city responsibilities versus other levels of government in managing specific negative externalities.

The industrial land use section of the bylaw could be expanded to include new land use districts that deal with specific planning areas. Using the examples of Vancouver and Victoria, specific geographic interface areas could be managed through identifying these specific areas as land use districts in the LUB. Policies now included in ARP documents could, in the future, become the foundation for new districts in the bylaw. New districts could be created for the different category interface areas, and inclusion in the LUB would enhance adherence to the policy. Three other possible new land use districts relevant to residential-industrial interfaces are described below.

5.2.5.1 *Transitional Business District*

Purpose- This district would permit industrial business operations that create no measurable nuisance levels according to the performance standards to locate adjacent to residential districts. The district shall also accommodate limited, compatible small-scale non-industrial uses. The district would serve to buffer residential districts from higher intensity industrial districts.

The Transitional Business District would be located at current category two and three interfaces. The district would be located at the periphery of other industrial districts and would effectively create a buffer between heavier industrial uses and adjacent land use areas. The Transitional Business District could function much like the proposed Industrial Interface Redevelopment Guidelines but would be embedded within the LUB instead of operating as a policy layer in addition to LUB regulations.

Two options are employable with regards to managing land use in the district. Firstly, all prospective uses could be made discretionary within the district. This would function in the same way as the current I-2 district that dictates all permitted uses become discretionary when located adjacent to a residential district, or PE district. Secondly, the City could outline very specific rules that limit the possible range of uses that are permitted and discretionary in the district. Clear quantifiable limits of activity would be included in the district.

5.2.5.2 *Live-Work Transition District*

Purpose- The live-work transition district would allow for residential and industrial land uses to exist in the same land use district provided the activity of industrial use did not adversely affect the health and well being of residents.

Several cities across Canada have explored the concept of live-work uses locating in mixed-use communities. The concept of mixed-use appears in the planning jargon as combining land uses that have been separated through the use of land use designations into areas and specific buildings that allow different uses to coexist. For Calgary, the idea of mixed-use tends to combine commercial and residential activity in the same building.[E] Calgary is a young city in comparison with most of the municipalities mentioned in Chapter Two, and the presence of older communities consisting of a wide variety of land uses is minimal. Inglewood and Ramsay are the only two communities within Calgary of any significant size that contain a significant eclectic mix of commercial, office, light industrial and residential uses.

The segregation of residential uses from all other uses, with the exception of institutional and a limited amount of commercial use, is fundamental to current land use management. The separation of uses that directly caused the squalor found in industrial cities was necessary. However, current zoning practices can stifle the creation of communities that contain the local mix of activities representative of human communities throughout history. Altering zoning regulations to allow a return to mixed-use areas will allow municipalities to create more interesting urban environments. This being stated, it is difficult to endorse the creation of a mixed-use industrial and residential area in Calgary because of the lack of mixed-use areas in the city. However, the possibility exists to include certain residential uses in an industrial transition district. Artist live-work studios, home businesses, and loft apartments catering to urbanites can coexist in industrial areas, even where a limited degree of noxious activities exist. "Today, there are many so-called 'clean' industries which are compatible with, and have the potential to be located within, residential areas."[13] Industry will likely never be accepted into Calgary's strictly suburban residential enclaves, but mixing industrial and residential uses, even within the same building, is possible at some interface areas.

Other cities across North America have experienced the creation of mixed-use areas in older industrial areas through the use of that area by the local art community. New York and San Francisco have experienced regeneration of older industrial areas spearheaded by local artisans looking for cheap, nondescript loft style spaces in which to conduct their business. In turn, these places became magnets for other related businesses, like bars and restaurants, and became trendy districts, attracting young urban professionals. The influx of higher income level residents drove up land prices forcing those that served as the impetus for the area's regeneration to vacate the area for more peripheral areas. New York and San Francisco have created policy to ensure these former industrial areas could accommodate residences but also drafted rules that protected area viability as an industrial district. This residential infiltration of industrial areas is not applicable to Calgary, instead commercial and office uses act as the drivers of land use price increases in Calgary's older industrial areas. If controlled properly, mixed-use transition districts, in the form of "residential-office districts can serve as a buffer between what would otherwise be conflicting land uses. By definition, they provide for a transition between residential and nonresidential uses."[14] The Manchester and Ogden ARPs employ this rationale in their live-work policy.

[E] Mixed-use development was a fact of life long before the advent of regulatory land use controls. The widespread adoption of land use controls in the 1920s and 30s compartmentalized almost every distinct use into separate districts. This was appropriate for certain high risk or nuisance producing land uses, but it also tore apart communities that evolved over time to accommodate vastly different uses that provided work, live, recreation, and community involvement opportunities within a small, well defined geographic area.

This paper has been concerned primarily with remedying land use conflicts in order to create communities in which current problems will subside. Accompanying the negative externalities that are found at residential-industrial interfaces are positive externalities that have been alluded to in this paper. Integrated mixed-use areas, of which residential and industrial uses are a part, create some of the liveliest and most interesting places in cities. These areas can provide affordable housing for those unable to afford housing in other areas. Housing in industrial areas can be of substandard quality or can occur as an illegal use in an inappropriate structure. However, the lower land costs provide an opportunity for government or housing co-operatives to establish affordable housing developments in these areas. Older industrial interface areas are home to dilapidated industrial buildings that, if redeveloped, provide opportunities to house work-live or loft style uses. Old warehouses with higher storey heights and older architectural adornments are ripe for conversion to lofts or business suites. Again, these buildings are limited to Inglewood and Ramsay and individual structures throughout Calgary.

The potential for implementing a live-work industrial district in Calgary is limited. Live-work policies can most effectively be implemented by inclusion in the Industrial Transition District Guidelines or Transitional Business District. Currently, work-live polices exist in Calgary ARPs and Direct Control districts. The Inglewood and Ramsay ARPs do not endorse any live-work policy, and the concept of live-work may yet be unpopular in Calgary. Providing live-work opportunities in Calgary may increase the feasibility of the concept as Calgary grows and people increasingly experience an urge to live in less secluded residential areas. "Having workplaces integrated with housing, schools, commercial streets and parks develops a sense of place and community that is noticeably absent in single-use neighbourhoods where it is necessary to commute long distances to work."[15] As transportation issues grow in importance in Calgary, people will increasingly desire an opportunity to live and work in the same community.

5.2.5.3 Traditional Industrial District

Purpose- "To preserve selected industrial areas for the accommodation of future traditional industrial use."[16]

The possibility exists in Calgary for the industrial uses within inner city industrial areas to be relocated to peripheral industrial areas, or to go out of business, because of an increase in property value. The Greenview Industrial Area (on the western edge of the Northeast Industrial Area) and the Central Industrial Area (see fig. 3.1), due to their location close to downtown, may be seen as sites for conversion to different land uses. Redevelopment as office or commercial uses might occur in industrial districts where industry is forced to suspend operation because of increases in property values. The inner city industrial areas provide a necessary commercial function for local businesses and residents. Relocating these industrial uses to the City's peripheral industrial areas may not be in the City's best interest considering the travel time required for all industrial needs to be met on the City's east side.

The industrial areas deemed most important to the City could be redesignated as Traditional Industrial Areas; with strict permitted use rules prohibiting uses that would cause a fundamental change to the land use area. Limiting acceptable land uses to industrial uses would ensure industrial operations could remain viable in the area. Interface specific policy would be included in the district regulations. The City of Calgary would need to identify the importance of retaining industrial areas in the inner city before deciding if the creation of this district is appropriate.

5.2.6 Industrial Interface Redevelopment Guidelines

Purpose- **The guidelines would encourage industrial development that is sensitive to existing neighbouring residential development in order to contribute to the community's character.**

The City of Calgary employs Low-Density Residential Housing Guidelines to manage infill development and additions and renovations to existing residential buildings in several inner city communities. The policies within the guidelines are designed to "encourage a variety of housing choices and sensitive infill redevelopment that contribute to the community's character and quality of life."[17] The guidelines are a City Council approved statutory document that applies to a large inner city geographic area. Guidelines could be created that apply to all industrial developments that are located next to residential land uses. Any industrial redevelopment or new development that is slated to occur next to a residential area, or within a predetermined distance, would be referred to the industrial interface redevelopment or infill guidelines to prescribe regulations for site development. Current ARPs already function to do this, but a citywide policy specific to interface development would standardize rules for all interfaces. The best policies used in existing ARPs could be applied to existing and future interfaces. Specific rules governing berming, fencing, landscaping, and architectural treatment would be covered in the guidelines to ensure that a specified level of quality development is attained. Performance based measures would best be included in the land use bylaw document. At this time, the City of Calgary prescribes that all I-2 industrial uses adjacent to residential areas are discretionary. This provision itself was included into the LUB in 2002 as a direct result of an industrial fire than occurred along the Fairview interface in 2001. The adoption of industrial infill guidelines would provide specific rules to both developers and planning staff to ensure the residential interface is dealt with across Calgary in a consistent fashion.

5.2.7 Visual Screening and Buffering Requirements

Purpose- **To provide specific development requirements for the interface between industrial developments and adjacent residential areas.**

Calgary citywide policy is ineffective at outlining the specific visual screening, berm, and landscape requirements that should be employed at interfaces. Many of the regulations state that the approving authority is to decide upon appropriate standards. Different from performance standards, the visual screening requirements could be included in a section of the land use bylaw. Table 2.1 is the matrix used by the City of Regina to determine what interface interventions are required at specific types of interfaces. The next step would be to determine specific types of visual screens, dividers, vegetation, and berm heights that would be used. These rules could be contained within the bylaw or any community scale policy, and are often used in ARP documents. However, these regulations would be most effective when included in an Industrial Interface Redevelopment Guideline document.

5.2.8 Industrial Area BRZ

Purpose- **To provide a means by which businesses located along a problematic residential-industrial interface can collect funds in order to enhance the quality of the interface.**

Businesses linked through location or activity commonly enter into business associations. As was disclosed in the interview with Jim Francisco industrial businesses have been reluctant in the past to consider entering into a Business Revitalization Zone association. The perceived benefits of a BRZ are seen as intended for businesses with a commercial or retail purpose looking to enhance the visual appearance of their area. BRZs act to pool money from individual businesses that will be used to improve the quality of the entire zone. Industrial business areas that experience significant negative interaction with local communities could use a BRZ programme to fund area improvements that could be initiated at the residential interface. These interventions would serve to improve the visual quality of the interface, possibly limit the escape of negative externalities from the industrial area, and most importantly to business owners, allow business to be conducted as normal without neighbour complaints. Service focused Industrial BRZs may benefit form the additional customers attracted to the area after the improvements are constructed. Improvements could include tree and vegetation planting, themed signage, sidewalk paving, site clean up, and painting of older buildings. The potential for reducing some of the nuisance conditions, including odour and noise, exists with the planting of trees or vegetation. Providing visual improvements to the interface, in comparison with the cost of relocation, is a cost-effective strategy for small-scale business that would make the industrial area a more appropriate neighbour.

5.3 Interface Policy Options and the Calgary Context

The different options for improving Calgary land use policy concerning residential-industrial interfaces are compared below. Figure 5.2 highlights which options are most appropriate for Calgary. The benefits and problems associated with adopting each system will be listed. The appropriateness of the policy option to the Calgary context will be rated, with those options achieving a 'yes' appropriateness rating warranting further comment in the concluding chapter.

Figure 5.2- Appropriateness of Interface Policy Options for Calgary

Option	Benefits	Problems	Appropriate To Calgary?
Continued Use of Existing Policy (5.2.1)	-no LUB rewrite required -development industry and City staff familiarity with the system	-problematic interfaces continue to exist in city as current policy is incapable of improving problem areas	**NO**- change to the current system is required
New Style Community Planning (5.2.2)	-reduce redundancy of policy by dealing with issues specific to larger geographic areas -rapid policy creation process -communities along the same interface can be grouped together	-not applicable to entire city	**PARTLY**- policies for groups of communities a step in the right direction
Performance Based Industrial Land Use Planning (5.2.3)	-provides industrial location flexibility -sets clear limits of negative externalities to be monitored -does not exclude yet to be developed industries -allows for mix of 'clean' industry with other uses	-not all externalities are easy to measure -requires inspection staff trained in performance monitoring -nature of industries change quickly- difficult to provide staff to monitor all industrial operations on consistent basis	**YES**- the current performance standards approach requires an update
Risk Based Land Use Planning (5.2.4)	-minimizes health and property damage risks	-difficult to implement in already built out areas -Risk Assessment another step in the development application process	**PARTLY**- large scale industrial activity is limited in Calgary-need for pure risk based planning greater in other cities
Land Use Bylaw Rewrite (5.2.5)	-provide Calgary with clearer rules pertaining to development of the interface -create new rules dictating which uses can locate adjacent to one another	-lengthy and precise process- interface issue one of a multitude of issues to be addressed -inclusion of too many interface regulations could make the new LUB unusable	**YES**- currently undertaken
Transitional Business District (5.2.5.1)	-provides limited list of uses that could locate along an interface -development guidelines would be embedded in the LUB	-requires significant land use redesignations across Calgary	**YES**- provides more detailed citywide policy

Live-work (5.2.5.2)	-provides flexibility in allowing new lifestyles -apply new uses to previously underdeveloped areas	-noxious effects may still occur at interfaces -residential uses may threaten existing industrial area with infiltration or complaints	**PARTLY**- new district unnecessary; policy can be included within transitional district policy
Traditional Industrial District (5.2.5.3)	-protect Calgary's vital inner city industrial areas from conversion to other uses	-may allow noxious effect producer to remain -may maintain the substandard quality of the residential interface -area is still productive and encouragement to redevelop may be nonexistent	**PARTLY**- conduct further study to determine long-term viability and need for inner city industrial areas
Industrial Interface Redevelopment Guidelines (5.2.6)	-apply to all interfaces -contains specific quantifiable guidelines for industrial development along interfaces	-another level of policy on top of existing ARPs, LUB, and Calgary Plan	**PARTLY**- prescriptive design rules would improve visual quality of interfaces
Visual Screening and Buffering Requirements (5.2.7)	-apply to all interfaces -outline exactly how visual quality of interface to be improved -will negate effect of some negative externalities (noise) -could be placed in LUB	-requires intensified enforcement -will not contain the most dangerous interface conditions	**YES**- clearer rules outlining screening are needed
Industrial Area BRZ (5.2.8)	-improve visual appearance of interface through local levy	-likely deemed to be inappropriate strategy by businessmen in industrial areas	**PARTLY**- provides method of collecting money for interface intervention

The preceding figure outlines that many of the policy options can be employed in Calgary to improve residential-industrial interface policy. The concluding chapter will recommend the policy direction the City of Calgary could adopt in order to appropriately address problematic residential-industrial interfaces.

5.4 Conclusion

Many of the issues associated with problematic residential-industrial interfaces can be solved through the adoption of strict land use measures. Restricting the manufacturing, processing and other uses associated with the production of negative externalities will not cause the immediate cessation of problems. However, market forces and the turnover of businesses in inner city industrial areas will contribute to the long-term removal of the land uses using the most dangerous materials or employing the most dangerous industrial practices. The use of specific regulations governing the type of intervention to be built between incompatible land uses will ensure that something is done to appease both businesses and residents at interfaces where long-term land use change at the interface is not supported by Calgary citywide policy. Current Calgary land use policy should be able to improve the situations at most problematic interfaces, but it does not. The lack of any significant intervention built or implemented along the Fairview interface is testament to this situation. The approving authority has experienced difficulty in consistently employing discretionary control to improve interface quality across Calgary, therefore more prescriptive land use regulations intended to clarify the management of land use at the interface are developed in the policy recommendations presented in the final chapter.

Notes

[1] Edmonton, 1995.
[2] MIACC, 1995.
[3] MIACC, 1995.
[4] Schwab, 1993.
[5] Farr, 2002.
[6] Edmonton, 1995.
[7] MIACC, 1997.
[8] MIACC, 1995.
[9] Ale, 1992.
[10] MIACC, 1995.
[11] MIACC, 1995.
[12] OECD, 1992.
[13] Nasmith, 1994.
[14] Davidson, 2000.
[15] Nasmith, 1994.
[16] Ottawa, 1994.
[17] Calgary, 1993.

Chapter 6
The New Residential-Industrial Interface Policy

6.1 The Need for a New Industrial Interface District

A new industrial district located at the interface between category 2 and 3 interface communities and adjacent industrial districts is to be created in this chapter. The areas to be demarcated within the new district at each interface could include formerly industrial and residential land. Each interface area would need to be further reviewed in greater detail to determine the exact boundaries of the new land use district. For most interface areas, the new land use district would apply to the length of the industrial district directly adjacent to the residential district. For example, the redesignation of the Fairview interface would include the strip of businesses located north of the alley, and would not include any residential areas. However, parts of the Forest Lawn residential area may be redesignated as part of the interface district as a catalyst to improving the quality of several dilapidated residences in the area. The district to be created recognizes the following assumptions:

1. The Calgary Plan is the preeminent plan for the City. New industrial interface policy will recognize that "the continued viability of existing businesses should be a prime consideration in the resolution of problems."[1]

2. Industry will continue to exist in the city where the nature of the industrial activity does not adversely affect adjacent incompatible districts.

3. Calgary policy is currently capable of remedying most incompatible interfaces. However, the lack of set guidelines creates a situation in which the approving authority has been inconsistent in applying discretionary authority to improve problematic interfaces.

4. The performance standards section of the bylaw is incomplete. The City of Calgary should incorporate mention of the toxic material inventory project conducted by the Calgary Fire Department in a revised industrial performance standards section.

5. The scale of industrial activity in Calgary is insufficient to necessitate a change to the Risk Based planning approaching being adopted by Edmonton.

The new industrial district was created to showcase how existing bylaw regulations could be improved without necessitating the creation of entirely new statutory policy working outside of the LUB. The following regulations are written using the format currently employed in the City of Calgary LUB. The policy is by no means an end product; instead it is intended to show how the redesign of certain parts of the existing LUB could be augmented to improve interface areas. Of course, the inclusion of any new land use district would need to comply with the format used for the entire bylaw, therefore the new district is written in the language of the current Calgary LUB. The policy will focus on industry produced conditions only; residentially produced conditions would be mentioned in the residential section of the LUB.

6.2 General Rules for Industrial Districts

1. INDUSTRIAL PERFORMANCE STANDARDS

a. PURPOSE

The purpose of employing performance standards in the land use management of industrial uses is:

　　i.　to permit potential nuisances to be identified
　　ii.　to ensure that all industrial uses will provide methods to protect on and off site uses from hazards and nuisances according to the performance standards included in this bylaw
　　iii.　to ensure all methods available for the purpose of nuisance control and elimination will be employed
　　iv.　to protect industries from arbitrary exclusion based solely on the nuisance production by any particular type of use in the past

b. APPLICATION

After the date of adoption of this bylaw:

　　i.　any new use, building or structure shall comply with all of the performance standards created in this section
　　ii.　any existing use, building or structure which is extended, enlarged, moved, structurally altered or reconstructed shall comply with all of the performance standers in this section
　　iii.　these performance standards shall be the minimum standards to be met and maintained by all uses
　　iv.　monitoring of hazardous materials on industrial sites will be conducted with the co-operation of the Calgary Fire Department
　　v.　the approving authority may require an applicant to submit verification that the conditions of any senior government authority having jurisdiction over any performance standard contained herein have been met
　　vi.　the approving authority may require an applicant to prepare and submit a Risk Assessment outlining contingency plans for on-site emergencies. The Risk Assessment will include on-site and off-site emergency evacuation plans for a worst-case disaster scenario. The Risk Assessment will consider the impact of the release of all dangerous materials stored on site.

c. RESPONSIBILITY FOR CONTROL OF NEGATIVE EXTERNALITIES

The following chart outlines the potential negative externalities that may be produced by an industrial use. Definitions of each negative externality are included in Part 1, section 4 of this bylaw (refer to Chapter Three of this paper). The level of government with jurisdiction over each particular externality and the relevant legislation will be provided.

Negative Externality	Level of Government Responsible	Applicable Legislation or Responsible Government Department
Air Pollution	Provincial	EPEA=
Blast Overpressure	Municipal	LUB≅
Broadcast Interference	Federal	CRTCΘ
Effluent	Provincial	EPEA
Fire and Explosive Hazards	Municipal	Fire Prevention Bylaw
Glare	Municipal	LUB
Heat and Humidity	Municipal	LUB
Litter	Municipal	Unsightly Premises Bylaw
Noise	Municipal	Noise Bylaw
Odour	Provincial	EPEA
On Street Parking	Municipal	Calgary Parking Authority
Outdoor Storage & Waste Disposal	Municipal	-Nuisance Bylaw -Minimum Maintenance Bylaw -Unsightly Premises Bylaw -Waste Bylaw
Particulate Matter	Provincial	EPEA
Radiation Emissions	Federal	AECBZ
Toxic & Hazardous Materials	Municipal	Calgary Fire Department
Traffic	Municipal	Transportation and Planning Policy
Undesirable Social Activity	Municipal	Calgary Police Service
Unsightly Properties	Municipal	-Nuisance Bylaw -Minimum Maintenance Bylaw -Unsightly Premises Bylaw
Vibration	Municipal	LUB
Water Quality Deterioration	Provincial	EPEA

=Environmental Protection and Enhancement Act
≅Land Use Bylaw
ΘCanadian Radio-Television and Telecommunications Commission
ZAtomic Energy Control Board

Any negative externality produced by industry NOT covered in the above chart will be under the jurisdiction of the appropriate level of government. If an unknown negative externality is experienced, responsibility for initial monitoring and management of the negative externality will rest with the Approving Authority until the matter is brought to the attention of the Province of Alberta.

d. LAND USE BYLAW MANAGED PERFORMANCE STANDARDS

The negative externalities that are to be managed via the Land Use Bylaw are outlined below. Other City of Calgary bylaw regulations shall be applied to negative externalities that are not listed below. The performance standards of the negative externalities that fall under the jurisdiction of the Land Use Bylaw are:

i. **Blast Overpressure**
The excess atmospheric pressure generated by blasting operations shall not exceed 0.5 pounds per square inch at the property line.[2]

ii. **Glare**
All on-site lighting shall be located, oriented, and shielded so as not to adversely affect residential properties.

iii. **Heat and Humidity**
Any perceptible heat and humidity is prohibited beyond the property line of the industrial use.

iv. **Vibration**
Any heavy vibrating equipment must be located at least 150 metres from the property line of the industrial use.

Steady-State Vibration Limits[3]		
Vibration Limit	Peak Particle Velocity (Inches per Second)	
	Daytime	Nighttime*
At a Residential District	0.03	0.01
At any other Land Use District	0.06	0.06

*nighttime limits shall be considered to prevail from 7:00 pm to 7:00 am.

The performance based industrial policy listed above is simple yet effective. Each conceivable negative externality is listed and the government agency responsible for policing the effects of the negative externality is listed. Those externalities not listed are to be addressed by the City administration in consultation with the province. The relevant Calgary bylaws already in place concerning specific adverse effects of industrial activity are referenced. The new policy calls for the use of a Risk Assessment to be employed to determine the level of potential hazard created by an industry during a worst case scenario emergency event. This is a powerful policy tool that may be used to disclose the types and quantities of hazardous, toxic, and explosive material on site. The Industrial Performance Standards described above will apply to all industrial districts in Calgary, including the new residential-industrial district area outlined below.

6.3 IR Light Industrial-Residential Interface District

1. PURPOSE

The purpose of this district is to provide for a limited set of uses that will limit the production of adverse effects experienced by land uses in, and adjacent to, the district. The IR district will serve as a mixed-use buffer between predominantly light industrial and residential districts.

2. PERMITTED USES

Artist studios	Offices
Athletic and recreational facilities	Parking areas and structures
Co-operative housing	Parks and playgrounds
Essential public services	Public and quasi-public buildings
Greenhouses and nurseries	Radio and television studios
Grocery stores	Restaurant/drinking establishments
Mechanical reproduction & printing establishments	Restaurants-food service only
	Take-out food services
Motion picture production facilities	Utilities
Movement or storage of materials, goods or products	Utility building
	Work-live residences

3. PERMITTED USE RULES

In addition to the General Rules for Industrial Districts, the following rules shall apply:

a. Co-operative Housing

The housing co-operatives shall be privately or publicly funded not-for-profit enterprises. Any co-operative housing project application would require an accompanying Risk Assessment for determining the potential for hazards to human health due to proximity to industrial uses.

b. Visual Screening and Buffer Requirements

Specific visual screening, buffer and berming requirements are required between this land use district and other districts.✦

✦ The visual screening and buffering chart is included to show that specific intervention can be included to remedy certain interface issues. The chart includes only a small amount of possible interventions between the IR district and other districts. Other City departments would need to be consulted to determine the appropriate size of walls, what type to construct, what plant species are appropriate, and many other specific situations. Current landscaping policies located in the general rules for industrial districts section of the LUB should be expanded to include specific appropriate species to use as screens. The presentation of this specific data was beyond the scope of this paper and should be compiled during the review of the industrial section of the LUB. The chart serves only to provide an example of how the specific rules governing the management of interfaces can be included in the bylaw instead of stating the interface is to be left to the discretion of the approving authority.

Adjacent Land Use District	Measured or Anticipated Negative Externality	Appropriate Intervention	Details
I-2	Noise	Sound Attenuation Wall	Concrete-2 metres high
Any Residential	Noise	Sound Attenuation Wall	Concrete-3 metres high
	Odour	Operation restrictions	Limit Hours of Business Operation to 7 am-9 pm
	Unsightly Properties	Covered Screen	Place slats in chain link fences
		Fence	Wood- 2 metres high
Any Commercial	Parking by nonresidents and businesspeople	Parking pass program	Restrict parking to residents and businesses through permit system

c. Work-Live Provisions

Units shall be intended for both dwelling and working use of the occupant only (without any outside employee) with the maximum allowable working area limited to 70% of the gross floor area of each unit. No use shall cause or create any negative externality (listed in the performance standard section) outside of the unit.

d. Front Yard

    i.   a minimum depth of 2 metres, or a depth equal to half the height of the principal building, whichever is greater

    ii.   for the purposes of this section, all street frontages shall be considered as front yards

e. Side Yard

A minimum width of 1.2 metres from each side yard except:

    i.   a minimum width of 6 metres, or a width equal to half the height of the principal building, whichever is greater, where a side yard abuts a residential district

    ii.   a minimum width of 6 metres where a side yard is used to provide vehicular access to the rear of a property which does not abut a residential district

    iii.   no side yard is required where a site does not abut a residential district and where the wall of a structure is built of material which normally would not require maintenance

f. Rear Yard

A minimum depth of 1.2 metres except:

      i.   a minimum depth of 6 metres, or a depth equal to half the height of the principal building, whichever is greater, where a rear yard abuts a residential district

      ii.   no rear yard is required where a site does not abut a residential district and where the wall of a structure is built of material which normally would not require maintenance

      iii.   no rear yard is required where the site abuts a terminating railway lead line and there is no need for a railway spur-line or where the spur-line is incorporated within a building

g. Building Height

A maximum of 20 metres.

h. Landscape Requirements

The following areas shall be landscaped:
      i.   all front yards to a minimum depth of 2 metres
      ii.   a strip adjacent to the front of the principal building, where loading does not occur, to an average depth of 2.5 metres
      iii.   all minimum required side yards between the front and rear of a principal building where they are not used for vehicular circulation
      iv.   all minimum required rear yards where the site abuts a residential district
      v.   all adjoining City boulevards

i. Outside Storage

Outside storage, including the storage of trucks and trailers, shall only be allowed on the sides of the building not directly adjacent to primarily (over 50% floor area) residential sites.

j. Garbage Storage

Garbage and waste material shall be stored in weatherproof and animal-proof containers in accordance with the Waste Bylaw and shall be visually screened from all adjacent sites and public thoroughfares.

k. Parking and Loading

Parking and loading is prohibited along yards adjacent to predominantly (over 50% floor area) residential sites and residential districts.

4. DISCRETIONARY USES

Billiard parlours
Bottle return depots
Child care facilities
Commercial schools
Custodial quarters
Entertainment establishments

Financial institutions
Liquor stores
Manufacturing
Outdoor café
Private clubs and organizations
Private schools

5. DISCRETIONARY USE RULES

In addition to the General Rules for Industrial Districts, the following rules shall apply:

a. Custodial Quarters

Custodial quarters shall be limited to one only for any industrial site and shall be part of a principal use building.

b. Manufacturing

Any development application for a manufacturing land use shall be accompanied by a Risk Assessment. Any significant change to an existing manufacturing industrial operation activity shall also be accompanied by a Risk Assessment.

The IR District will provide specific regulations governing the treatment of the problematic interfaces between residential and industrial districts. The adoption of any land use bylaw change, especially the adoption of a new district, is open to significant debate. However, the recommendation is not intended as a wholesale fix-all; adopting any of the new policies in the recommendation is a move towards the eventual improvement of problematic interfaces.

6.4 Conclusion

The performance standards section and the new IR Light Industrial-Residential Interface District have attempted to provide land use strategies for improving problematic residential-industrial interfaces. The key recommendations included in the new policies include:

1. **Hazardous material monitoring is to be conducted jointly with the Calgary Fire Department.**

   The Fire Department is in the process of developing an inventory of hazardous, toxic, and potentially dangerous materials stored at industrial sites across Calgary. This inventory can be used by the City to gauge the need for developing further planning policy interventions at high-risk interfaces.

2. **The approving authority may require an applicant to prepare and submit a Risk Assessment.**

   The Risk Assessment process should disclose the potential for damage in the event of an industrial accident and inform the approving authority of the scale of the proposed industrial operation.

3. **Performance Standard responsibility is clearly established.**

   The inclusion of the chart outlining exactly which level of government (and associated policy) is responsible for each particular negative externality will clarify confusion of jurisdictional responsibility.

4. **Specific Performance Standards are developed.**

   For the negative externalities not addressed in other City of Calgary Bylaws, the performance standards, in the form of quantifiable limits, are included in the LUB.

5. **The permitted use list is limited.**

   The industrial uses that most commonly create adverse conditions for adjacent residential districts have been excluded from the IR district.

6. **Residential opportunities are permitted.**

   Work-live and co-operative housing opportunities are permitted in the IR district.

7. **Specific visual screening and buffering requirements are outlined.**

   The provision of screening and buffers is no longer a discretional decision of the approving authority. Placing strict guidelines for screens and buffers in the bylaw will ensure that the approving authority employs a minimum level of consistency.

8. Parking and storage on industrial sites is prohibited adjacent to residential sites.

The storage and movement of large industrial vehicles is not permitted in side and rear yards adjacent to residences.

9. Manufacturing is a discretionary use.

Not only will all prospective manufacturing land uses in the IR district be considered discretionary, but all new development applications for a manufacturing use must be accompanied by a Risk Assessment that will consider the effect of industrial operations on adjacent land uses. Significant changes to existing manufacturing operations will also require the preparation of a Risk Assessment.

This paper has focused almost exclusively on policy improvements and not procedure, although, ultimately, one cannot be separated form the other. Policy is only as effective as the rigour used in its implementation. Not only must the development process be adhered to stringently for all problematic interfaces to be significantly improved, but the political will must also exist if planning interventions are to be adopted. The impending rewrite of the Calgary Land Use Bylaw represents the political desire to modernize the regulations governing land use. Accompanying this rewrite should be the inclusion of policy recommendations highlighted in this paper. With each significant industrial incident that occurs at a residential-industrial interface, the political and popular will grows for something to be done at these areas. The recommendations can be used to improve compatibility of the existing uses at current interfaces and provide a district that can be used to prohibit new problematic interfaces from developing. A disaster of the magnitude of the Hub Oil fire should never occur, and the rethinking of the policies used to manage residential-industrial interfaces presented in this paper will aid in creating interfaces safe for both businesspeople and residents.

6.5   Planning Over the Edge: Opportunities for Further Research

Any exercise of academic study encounters difficulties at every step in the process in refining the scope of the work. There are always questions that go unanswered, queries that are only mentioned in passing, and inquiries that can only be hinted at for future pursuit. Several opportunities abound in employing this research as a guide for further development of interface related research.

1. The edge as the third place.

Purposefully, the focus of this research project did not stray from the restraints of the real world Calgary planning context. A possible research outgrowth of this paper would be an examination of the interface between two distinct districts as a place unto itself. The work of Richard Foreman, noted for his landscape ecology theory work highlighted in could be applied to residential-industrial interfaces in order to create typologies of interfaces based on their shapes, widths, thickness and mixes of use.

2. The edge as community.

The boundary between the industrial and residential districts may be the point at which community is formed. Instead of acting as a partition, this interface may represent where traditional communities engage in social and community activity. Opportunity exists to highlight these connections and avoid the separation of uses, even if at first glance they appear to be exclusively problematic. The interface may be the synthesis of two different districts creating a positive externality where social, economic, and cultural interaction flourish.

3. Specific recommendations for different interface typologies.

Instead of creating a list of general policy recommendations, specific recommendations could be developed for the three different categories of interfaces described in Chapter Three.

4. Expand the review of other municipal policy.

Include the comparison of interface policies employed by American and other international cities that employ far different approaches to interface planning. The focus could range from smaller urban municipalities that employ specific industrial interface policy to semi-urban or rural areas that employ unique industrial interface policy.

5. Implications for design.

A logical next step is to apply the policy recommendations to physical interface design. The communities of Inglewood and Ramsay could be selected as areas appropriate for exploration of design interventions. Design concepts could be conceived at different scales of environmental design. The planner would be interested in designing the interface community while the environmental scientist may be interested in exploring the opportunities for eco-industrial adaptation of the interface. The architect may be interested in applying recommendations to interface building design when the industrial designer may be inspired by opportunities to design specific structures along the interface. The opportunity exists for other Environmental Design disciplines to expand the planning recommendations herein and create new and diverse places not yet found, or even considered, in Calgary or other cities around the world.

Notes

[1] Calgary, 1998.
[2] Schwab, 1993.
[3] North Riverside, 1993.

Appendix A

Zoning and Development Control in the City of Calgary

- July 23, 1934   Zoning bylaw 2835 enacted
- March 1, 1952   Zoning bylaw 4271 (interim) approved
- June 19, 1953   Zoning bylaw 4916 approved
- February 4, 1969   Zoning bylaw 7500 approved
- March 16, 1970   Development Control bylaw 7839 approved
- May 29, 1972   Development control bylaw 8600 approved
- March 31, 1980   Land Use bylaw approved

There were also two development control bylaws, 5997 and 8011, that regulated portions of the City of Calgary.

Appendix B

Edmonton Industrial Interface Policy

Plan Edmonton: Edmonton's Municipal Development Plan

The following policies deal with the residential-industrial interfaces:

- Address compatibility of land use in the development and review of land use plans and development proposals (Policy 1.1.2).

- Develop strategies to focus heavy industrial land development [in identified areas in the plan] (Policy 1.1.4).

- Address adequate separation distances and effective transition zones between heavy industry and other uses through a risk management approach based on the principles of:

- Risk reduction at source;
- Risk reduction through land use controls;
- Emergency preparedness;
- Risk communication (Policy 1.1.6).

Maintain and improve older commercial and industrial areas while mitigating negative impacts on adjacent neighbourhoods (Policy 1.5.4).

Edmonton Zoning Bylaw 2001

- **Industrial Zone General Purpose** (Section 400.1). The purpose of this Zone is to provide for a wide range of Industrial Uses in conjunction with an Industrial Statutory Plan, where uses are based on assessments of their on-site and-site development impacts and their ability to deal with those impacts, as set out in the regulations of this Bylaw and the requirements of an Industrial Statutory Plan.

- **General Development Regulations for Industrial Zones** (Section 400.3). The following regulations shall apply to any development, except where altered by either Section 400.4 or an Industrial Plan Overlay: no activity or operation shall cause, or permit to be caused, a noise level at or inside the boundary line of a Residential Zone that exceeds the regulations of the Noise Abatement Bylaw.

- **Development Regulations for Sensitive or Special Areas** (Section 400.4). Sensitive or special areas include sites abutting or adjacent to a Residential Zone. In this section, the bylaw prescribes rules for all industrial sites adjacent to a Residential Zones, including floor area ratio limits, height and yard restrictions. There is also provision for appearance standards, including:

    - carrying out all activities in an enclosed building and restricting outdoor display areas

- locating all loading, service, trash collection and Accessory storage areas, and trucking yards to the rear or sides of the principal building and screening this activity via walls, landscape materials, berms, fences, or a combination of these, to the satisfaction of the Development Officer
- requiring, at the behest of the Development Officer, exposed projections outside the building to be screened if such projections are inconsistent with the character and appearance of surrounding developments or the intended visual qualities of this zone.

- **(IB) Industrial Business Zone** (Section 410). The general purpose of this zone is to provide for industrial businesses that carry out their operations such that no nuisance is created or apparent outside an enclosed building and such that the Zone is compatible with any adjacent non-industrial Zone, and to accommodate limited, compatible non-industrial businesses. This zone should normally be located on the periphery of industrial areas and adjacent to arterial or major collector roadways.

- **(IM) Medium Industrial Zone** (Section 420). This Zone should normally be applied on the interior of industrial areas adjacent to collector and local industrial public roadways such that Uses are separated from any adjacent residential areas by a higher quality Industrial or Commercial Zone.

- **(IH) Heavy Industrial Zone** (Section 430). The general purpose of this zone is to provide for Industrial Uses that, due to their appearance, noise, odour, risk of toxic emissions, or fire and explosion hazards are incompatible with residential, commercial, and other land uses.

- **(IS) Special Industrial Zone** (Section 440). The purpose of this Zone is to provide for special industrial Uses in such a manner to create an attractive environment characterized by quality in architectural design, site planning and landscaping, where land Uses do not create or cause undesirable off-site impacts.

Appendices

Appendix C

Sound Levels and Human Response (source: City of Calgary Noise Bylaw)

Common Sounds	Noise Level dB(A)	Effect on Humans
Air raid siren	130	
Jet takeoff (200 ft.)	120	Threshold of pain
Amplified rock music	110	Maximum vocal effort
Jet takeoff (2000 ft.)	100	
Jackhammer	88-99	
Lawn mower (right at the source – 0 ft.)	93	
Loud shout	90	
Many industrial work places	85	Level at which hearing damage begins (after 8 hours of exposure)
Busy traffic intersection	80	
Noisy restaurant	70	Interferes with telephone conversation, steady sound becomes annoying
Noisy office, normal conversation at 3 ft.	60	Intrusive
Quiet street inside average urban home	50	
Public Library	40	Quiet
Soft whisper at 5 ft.	30	Very quiet
Normal breathing	10	Just audible

The Noise Bylaw prohibits any disturbing noise from construction work and related activities, including demolishing, erecting, altering or repairing any building or landscaping in a residential development between 10 p.m. and 7 a.m. Monday-Saturday and between 10 p.m. and 9 a.m. Sundays and statutory holidays.

How is sound measured?
Sound level information is recorded in the decibel scale (dB), which is based on logarithms. The logarithmic scale means that an increase of 10 dB actually increases the sound energy 10 times. However, because of the way the human ear perceives sound, this increase of 10 dB is only perceived as being twice as "loud." Sound measured with a sound level meter is usually expressed as dBA. The 'A' weighting network filters the signal to produce a reasonably accurate representation of human perception of sound.

Leq Measurements
To deal with constant, fluctuating and non-continuous sound levels, the Noise Bylaw describes them in terms of the equivalent continuous sound level (Leq). 'Leq' is the steady sound level over a specified period of time that has the same acoustic energy as the fluctuating sound during that period. Leq measurements are made over 15 minute, 1-hour or 2-hour periods. The meter continuously measures and records fluctuating sound levels over the appropriate time period. It calculates the Leq and then produces a single number that approximates the "average," or the equivalent continuous sound level.

Appendix D

Hamilton Industrial Interface Policy

Hamilton Zoning Bylaw 1980

- **Area Requirements-** In a J district, coverage by buildings and structures shall not exceed eighty-five per cent of the area of the lot, provided that where any side lot line or rear lot line abuts upon a residential district, no building or structure shall be located nearer to any such side lot line or rear lot line than 4.5 metres (14.76 feet). (Section 16-J Districts).

- **Area Requirements** as above, and no rear yard shall be required except where a rear lot line abuts upon a residential district, when there shall be a rear yard of a width of at least 6.0 metres (19.69 feet). (Section 16A-JJ Districts).

Appendix E

Ottawa Industrial Interface Policy

Ottawa Regional Plan 1999

- **Contaminated Sites** (Section 11.4) states that Council shall:

    - Define contaminated sites as sites where the environmental condition of the property and the quality of the soil or groundwater, particularly on former industrial or waste-disposal sites, may have the potential for adverse effects to human health or the natural environment.

    - When reviewing development applications, require that the applicant indicate that they have completed a phase 1 Environmental Site Assessment and are satisfied that there is no evidence of contamination on the site.

    - The Site Assessment process involves undertaking a Historical Land Use Survey, in co-operation with the area municipalities, utility companies and the Ministry of the Environment and Energy, to identify areas of potential contamination. A Historical Land use survey is a systematic collection of information on the type and location of past land uses that could have caused contamination of soil or groundwater.

- **Policies For Noise** (Section 11.6). According to the Plan, different types of noise are dealt with separately because they are measured and regulated differently.

City of Ottawa Official Plan 1994

- **Traditional Industrial Areas** (Section 4.5) are intended to:

    - preserve selected industrial areas for the accommodation of traditional industrial uses
    - increase the viability of traditional industrial areas by exercising strict control over the amount of non-industrial activity permitted in these locations
    - encourage the relocation or upgrading of industrial uses in locations not designated as Traditional Industrial Areas, where such uses impact negatively upon adjacent industrial uses

The policies established in the Ottawa Plan (Policy 4.5.1) for this zone include:

- permitting a mix of low density, traditional industrial uses in areas designated as Traditional Industrial Areas. Permitted uses may include manufacturing, warehouse and distribution uses, communications, utilities and transportation, storage, construction, related personal service/convenience uses and recreational uses. These [traditional industrial] uses provide supplies and services to the city's dominant office and commercial economy, the advanced technology sector and local consumer market

and may have the potential to impact negatively on the community in terms of noise, fumes, or visual appearance.
- when considering proposals for new development or expansions to existing development within the Traditional Industrial Areas, industrial uses or development shall not be permitted which is considered to represent a significant health or safety risk to its citizens or the environment by reason of noise pollution of the environment, or by virtue of any other adverse environmental impact.

- City Council shall support the relocation of older industrial uses from areas not designated as Traditional Industrial Area where the uses are not compatible with those uses located in adjacent areas.

Appendix F

Regina Industrial Interface Policy

Regina Zoning Bylaw

- **Zone IIT: The Innismore Industrial Transitional Zone** is intended to provide the wide range of industrial and manufacturing uses typically found in an industrial zone but exclude those industries which may be offensive by reason of noise, smell or other forms of pollution.

- **Noise** (Section 9.12) states that no sound shall be emitted from any building, structure or land or from any operation thereon that exceeds the standards identified...when measured at any point on the boundary of the site.

- **Obnoxious Use** (Section 9.13), states that no use shall be conducted to emit any obnoxious or dangerous degree of heat, glare, radiation, fumes, odour, or dust beyond the lot lines of the lot containing the use.

- **Landscape and Buffer Regulations** (Section 15) are intended to:
    - provide minimum landscape requirements for developed lots, streets and street frontages, parking areas, open spaces, buffer areas, visual screens, and major roadway landscape design areas in order to facilitate the creation of an attractive and harmonious streetscape
    - mitigates pollution by contributing to the process of air purification, oxygen regeneration and groundwater recharge
    - mitigate incompatible land uses by requiring a screen or buffer to minimize the visual or lighting impacts of an adjoining or nearby use.

- **Visual Screening and Buffering** (Section 15C), includes regulations intended to:
    - separate different land uses from each other
    - eliminate or minimize potential nuisances such as dirt, litter, noise, and glare
    - separate unsightly land uses
    - provide spacing to reduce adverse impacts of noise, odour, or dangers from fire or explosion

Appendix G

Saskatoon Industrial Interface Policy

Saskatoon Development Plan 1998

- **Industrial Land Use Policies** (Section 7.1) Where industrial uses are considered incompatible with residential uses, they shall be segregated wherever possible, and in such cases screening by landscaping, buffer strips, berming or separation by transitional use may be required.

- **Business Park** (Section 7.2). Business Park uses shall not create land use conflicts related to smoke, noise, vibration, dust, odour or potential environmental contamination during their normal course of operations, and therefore, may be located adjacent to residential areas. The physical design of Business Parks shall include an overall quality of site development that is superior to Light or Heavy Industrial areas.

- **Light Industrial** (Section 7.3). Light Industrial land uses shall not normally create land use conflicts due to excessive noise, vibration, dust, smoke, or odour. As a result, Light Industrial areas may be located adjacent to residential areas, although some form of buffering may be required.

    - Light Industrial lands may act as a buffer or transitional area between more intensive industrial uses and incompatible uses, such as residential areas.

- **Heavy Industrial** (Section 7.4). Relevant policies include:

    - Heavy industrial areas should not normally be situated adjacent to Residential or Business Park land use designations.
    - Heavy Industrial areas shall generally be well removed from residential areas and concentrated in a minimal number of separate locations.
    - In order to minimize land use conflicts between existing Heavy Industrial areas and nearby Residential Areas, the redesignation of Heavy Industrial areas to other land use classifications shall be encouraged as opportunities present themselves.

Saskatoon Zoning Bylaw No. 6772, 1987

- **IL1- General Light Industrial District.** The purpose is to facilitate economic development through a wide variety of light industrial activities and related businesses that do not create land use conflicts or nuisance conditions during the normal course of operations.

- **IL2- Limited Intensity Light Industrial District.** The purpose is to facilitate economic development through certain light industrial activities and related businesses that do not create land use conflicts or nuisance conditions during the normal course of operations, as well as to limit activities oriented to public assembly.

- **IB- Industrial Business District.** The purpose is to facilitate business and light industrial activities that are seeking a high quality, comprehensively planned environment.

- **IH- Heavy Industrial District.** The purpose is to facilitate economic development through industrial activities that may have potential for creating nuisance conditions during the normal course of operations.

- **AM- Auto Mall District.** The purpose is to provide for motor vehicle sales and service and other directly related uses in high quality, comprehensively planned environments which are conveniently located to serve automobile customers.

- **Holding Symbol 'H'.** The Purpose is to identify areas within the City limits where the future use of land or the timing of development is uncertain due to issues of servicing, transitional use, or market demand.

- **RA- Reinvestment Area District (Proposed).** This is a mixed-use zone, which will combine commercial, residential, and light industrial use.

Municipal Enterprise Zones in Saskatoon, 2002 Discussion Paper

The discussion paper proposes possible incentives that may encourage improvements in Municipal Enterprise Zones, including:

- Building Permit Fee Waiver or Rebate. This may include new construction and renovation work for both commercial and residential uses.
- Building Code Equivalencies- Redevelopment may not be as expensive as some owners think.
- Relocation Assistance/Land Swapping- Due to historical circumstances, there are unsightly and potentially dangerous industrial uses adjacent to residential areas. The City will offer a land swapping or relocation incentive to encourage old industrial uses to relocate to newer, planned industrial subdivisions within Saskatoon.

Appendix H

Toronto Industrial Interface Policy

Toronto Official Plan Part 1, 1987

- **Restricted Industrial Areas** (Section 4.17). Restricted Industrial Areas shall be regarded as areas containing a limited range of industrial uses which are environmentally compatible with adjacent residential or commercial areas.

- **Mixed Industrial-Residential Area** (Section 4.23). Mixed Industrial-Residential Areas shall be regarded as areas containing a mix of a wide range of residential uses, community services and facilities, street-related retail and service uses, and those industrial uses which are environmentally compatible with adjacent and neighbouring uses.

    - Council shall pass bylaws to restrict industrial uses permitted in Mixed Industrial-Residential Areas to those which are normally environmentally compatible with adjacent and neighbouring residential uses in terms of emissions, odour, noise and generation of traffic.

    - Council is satisfied that the design of mixed-use industrial-residential buildings, has taken into account factors such as: the appropriate separation of areas of car and truck activity from areas of pedestrian activity; the provision of an adequate number of parking spaces for workers, visitors, and residents; the provision of adequate residential amenities; the provision of a satisfactory noise environment for both residents and workers; and the satisfaction of appropriate environmental standards for industrial uses contained in such buildings.

    - Prior to passing bylaws to permit a change in use, Council shall have regard for the extent to which the change would adversely affect the continued compatibility of neighbouring uses, particularly in those areas where identifiable pockets of a consistent use, industrial or residential, exist.

Toronto Official Plan Summary, 2002

- Scattered throughout many **Neighbourhoods** are sites of former non-residential uses such as an industry, institution, retail store, or utility corridor. In converting these sites to residential uses, there is a genuine opportunity to add to the quality of Neighbourhood life.

- **Regeneration Areas** open up unique areas of the city to a wide range of uses to attract investment and spur growth. In Regeneration Areas, commercial, residential, live/work, institutional and light industrial uses can be mixed within the same block or even the same building. Not all Regeneration Areas will have the same mix of uses or development policies. Each will differ in terms of its existing built context, character of adjacent areas and market opportunities for revitalization. Regeneration Areas will need 'tailor-made' strategies and frameworks for development provided through a Secondary Plan. In some cases, there will be a need for extensive infrastructure improvements, in others the emphasis will be on the re-use of existing buildings and compatible infill. But, in every case Regeneration Areas represent a tremendous opportunity to unlock potential and help direct growth within the city.

Appendices

Appendix I

Vancouver Industrial Interface Policy

Vancouver CityPlan, 1995

- **Diverse Economy and Jobs Close to Home.** Industrial lands will be maintained for all new types of industries and businesses; high tech research, repair services, and warehouses located near their customers and workers. Challenges associated with achieving this policy goal include:

    - Attracting suitable businesses to neighbourhood centres.
    - Reversing the trend of allowing housing and retail development to replace industry.

Vancouver Zoning and Development Bylaw No. 3575

- **MC-1 and MC-2 Districts.** The purpose is to reinforce the mixed use nature of this area, with residential, commercial, and light industrial uses permitted. Emphasis is placed on building design that furthers compatibility among uses, and contributes to area character and pedestrian interest. The MC-2 District differs from the MC-1 District in limiting dwelling uses in areas adjacent to a heavy impact industrial zone.

- **M-1, M1-A, M-2, and I-2 Districts** are intended to permit industrial and other uses that are generally incompatible with residential land use. It is not the intent, however, to permit uses that are potentially dangerous or environmentally incompatible when situated near residential districts.

- **M-1B District.** This district is intended to provide an industrial district schedule that permits industrial and other related uses under conditions designed to minimize conflicts with adjacent or nearby residential uses. This district is also intended to discourage uses that are not related to the industrial sector.

- **IC-1 and IC-2 District.** The primary intent is to permit light industrial uses that are generally compatible with one another and with adjoining residential or commercial districts. It is also the intent to permit advanced technology industry, industry with a significant amount of research and development activity, and commercial uses compatible with and complementing light industrial uses.

- **IC-3 District.** The purpose is to permit a mix of light industrial, live arts and theatre, residential and related uses that are generally compatible with adjoining residential and commercial districts. Service uses compatible with and complementing light industrial uses and a limited number of office uses are also permitted, but not general retail stores.

- **I-1 District** is intended to permit light industrial uses that are generally compatible with one another and with adjoining residential or commercial districts.

- **I-3 District.** The intent is to permit high technology industry, and industry with a significant amount of research and development activity. It is also the intent to permit light industrial uses that are generally compatible with one another and with adjoining residential or commercial districts.

Appendix J

Victoria Industrial Interface Policy

Victoria Official Regional Plan 1974

- **Industrial Conversion Areas** are designated lands within Established Industrial Areas that because of encroachment by non-industrial uses are not currently available for industrial uses but that have:

    - Established adjacent industrial uses
    - Existing or imminent services
    - Strategic proximity for regional transportation facilities that are suitable for conversion back to industrial use through removal of non-industrial uses.

Victoria Zoning Bylaw 1999

- **M-1 Zone, Limited Light Industrial District** (Section 7.1). The purpose of this district is to:
    - permit limited light industrial uses, excluding manufacturing, processing and assembly, that are generally compatible with one another
    - permit as uses "high tech", "work-live", service-commercial, and limited retail uses that are compatible and complementary to limited light industrial uses.

- **M-2 Zone, Light Industrial District** (Section 7.2).

- **M2-I Zone, Douglas-Blanshard Industrial District** (Section 7.2.1). The purpose of this zone is to:
    - permit limited light industrial uses, including manufacturing, processing and assembly, that are generally compatible with one another, and
    - permit as uses "high tech", "work live", service-commercial, and limited retail uses that are compatible and complementary to limited light industrial uses

- **M-3 Zone, Heavy Industrial District (Section 7.3) and S-1 Zone, Limited Service District (Section 7.6)**

Appendix K

Winnipeg Industrial Interface Policy

Plan Winnipeg 2001

- **Implement an Industrial Land Planning Strategy** (Policy 2C-04). This would be accomplished by determining the best strategic sites for industry property developments while ensuring compatibility with environmental regulations, existing industrial developments, residential areas, and available infrastructure.

- **Promote Vibrant Neighbourhoods** (Policy 3B-01). This policy calls for the city to promote vibrant neighbourhoods by encouraging and accommodating within new and existing development a variety of compatible mixed uses.

- **Accommodating New Industrial Areas** (Policy 3B-06). New industrial areas will be developed, but first the city will:

    - evaluate new industrial development proposals to ensure that existing neighbourhoods are protected
    - allow the possible introduction of commercial uses in industrial areas to act as a buffer between the industrial uses and adjacent uses or to service the needs of the local industrial population.

- **Provide Ongoing Stewardship of Industrial Areas** (Policy 3B-07). This will be done to promote the long-term viability of industrial areas and minimize land use conflicts by evaluating new residential development proposals to ensure that existing industrial operations in the vicinity are protected.

- **Addresses Water, Air, and Noise Pollution** (Policy 5A-05). This policy specifies that the city shall address water, air, and noise pollution by protecting residential developments from the adverse impacts of air pollution sources, including stubble and other burning.

Winnipeg Zoning Bylaw

Zoning layers as outlined in the Downtown Winnipeg Zoning Bylaw:

- residential land use
- non residential land use
- bulk
- parking and loading
- signs
- urban design

Appendices

The zones of The City of Winnipeg Zoning Bylaw regulate:

- permitted uses;
- size (bulk) of the buildings permitted in relation to the size of the lot;
- the maximum amount of building coverage allowed on the lot;
- the distance between the building and the lot line;
- the amount of parking required; and other requirements including the size and placement of signs.

Appendix L

Communities of Calgary

Abbeydale	Downtown East Village	Martindale	Shawnee Slopes
Acadia	Downtown West End	Mayfair	Shawnessy
Albert Park/Radisson Heights	Eagle Ridge	Mayland	Shepard Industrial
Altadore	East Fairview Industrial	Mayland Heights	Signal Hill
Alyth/Bonnybrook	East Shepard Industrial	McCall	Silver Springs
Applewood Park	Eastfield	McKenzie Lake	Skyline East
Arbour Lake	Eau Claire	McKenzie Towne	Skyline West
Aspen Woods	Edgemont	Meadowlark Park	Somerset
Banff Trail	Elbow Park	Meridian	South Airways
Bankview	Elboya	Midnapore	South Calgary
Bayview	Erin Woods	Millrise	South Foothills
Beddington Heights	Erlton Woods	Mission	Southview
Bel-Aire	Evanston	Monterey Park	Southwood
Bonavista Downs	Evergreen	Montgomery	Springbank Hill
Bowness	Fairview	Mount Pleasant	Spruce Cliff
Braeside	Fairview Industrial	New Brighton	St. Andrews Heights
Brentwood	Falconridge	North Airways	Starfield
Bridgeland/Riverside	Fish Creek Park	North Glenmore Park	Stoney 1
Bridlewood	Foothills	North Haven	Stoney 2
Britannia	Forest Heights	North Haven Upper	Stoney 3
Burns Industrial	Forest Lawn	Nose Hill Park	Stoney 4
Calgary International Airport	Forest Lawn Industrial	Oakridge	Strathcona Park
Cambrian Heights	Franklin	Ogden	Sunalta
Canada Olympic Park	Glamorgan	Ogden Shops	Sundance
Canyon Meadows	Glenbrook	Palliser	Sunnyside
Capitol Hill	Glendale	Panorama Hills	Sunridge
Castleridge	Glendeer Business Park	Parkdale	Symons Valley
Cedarbrae	Glenmore Park	Parkhill/Stanley Park	Taradale
CFB – Currie	Golden Triangle	Parkland	Temple
CFB – Lincoln Park PMQ	Great Plains	Patterson	Thorncliffe
Chaparral	Greenview	Pegasus	Tuscany
Charleswood	Greenview Industrial Park	Penbrooke Meadows	Tuxedo Park
Chinatown	Greenwood/Greenbriar	Pineridge	University Heights
Chinook Park	Hamptons	Point McKay	University of Calgary
Christie Park	Harvest Hills	Pump Hill	Upper Mount Royal
Cinnamon Hills	Harvest Hills Business Park	Queens Park Village	Valley Ridge
Citadel	Hawkwood	Queensland	Valleyfield
Cliff Bungalow	Haysboro	Ramsay	Varsity
Coach Hill	Hidden Valley	Ranchlands	Victoria Park
Collingwood	Highfield	Red Carpet/Mountview	Vista Heights
Connaught	Highland Park	Renfrew	West Hillhurst
Copperfield	Highwood	Richmond	West Springs
Coral Springs	Hillhurst	Rideau Park	Westgate
Cougar Ridge	Horizon	Riverbend	Westwinds
Country Hills	Hounsfield Heights/Briar Hill	Rocky Ridge	Whitehorn
Country Hills Village	Huntington Hills	Rosedale	Wildwood
Coventry Hills	Inglewood	Rosemont	Willow Park
Cranston	Kelvin Grove	Rosscarrock	Windsor Park
Crescent Heights	Killarney/Glengarry	Roxboro	Winston Heights/Mountview
Crestmont	Kingsland	Royal Oak	Woodbine
Dalhousie	Lake Bonavista	Rundle	Woodlands
Deer Ridge	Lakeview	Rutland Park	
Deer Run	Lincoln Park Redevelopment	Saddle Ridge	
Deerfoot Business Centre	Lower Mount Royal	Saddle Ridge Industrial	
Diamond Cove	Macewan Glen	Sandstone Valley	
Discovery Ridge	Manchester	Scarboro	
Douglas Glen	Manchester Industrial	Scarboro/Sunalta West	
Douglasdale Estates	Maple Ridge	Scenic Acres	
Dover	Marlborough	Section 23	
Downtown Commercial Core	Marlborough Park	Shaganappi	

Appendix M

Municipal and Industrial Activities Where Hazardous Substances May Be Found (source: MIACC, 1997).

Airports
Barges (marine)
Chemical plants
Colleges
Compressed gas dealers
Compressed gas facilities
Construction sites
Construction yards
Curling rinks
Electrical generation facilities
Explosive magazines
Farm supply dealers
Fertilizer dealers
Fertilizer manufacturers
Food processing plants
Food storage facilities
Gas plants
Government facilities
Hockey rinks
Hospitals
Hotels
Labs
Leather tanning facilities
Machine shops
Manufacturing facilities
Marine terminals
Medical labs
Mining operations
Non-destructive testing companies
Nuclear facilities
Oil well logging companies
Oil well servicing companies
Paper mills
Pharmacological manufacturers
Plastic manufacturers
Plating processing
Printing plants
Pipeline operators
Rail lines
Rail sidings and yards
Refineries
School labs
Sewerage treatment facilities
Ship facilities
Storage facilities
Swimming pools
Tank farms
Textile plants
Trucking corridors
Truck stops
Trucking terminals
Universities
Waste storage facilities
Waste treatment facilities
Waterfront facilities
Warehouses
Water slides
Water treatment facilities
Welding shops
Wood preservation operations
Yeast production plants

Appendix N

Abbreviations Used in Tables 3.1-3.4

LUD- Land Use Designation
- A   Agricultural and Open Space District
- C-1A   Local Commercial District
- C-3   General Commercial District
- C-5   Shopping Centre Commercial District
- C-6   Highway Commercial District
- DC   Direct Control District
- I-2   General Light Industrial District
- I-3   Heavy Industrial District
- I-4   Limited-Serviced Industrial District
- PE   Public Park, School and Recreation District
- PS   Public Service District
- R-1   Residential Single-Detached District
- R-1A   Residential Narrow Lot Single-Detached District
- R-2   Residential Low Density District
- RM-1   Residential Low Density Multi-Dwelling District
- RM-4   Residential Medium Density Multi-Dwelling District
- UNR   University Research District
- UR   Urban Reserve District

BP-Business Park
CP-Canadian Pacific
SFD-Single Family Dwellings

Appendix O

Interview Guide

Interviewer: Jaydan Tait
Participant:

The purpose of this interview is to chronicle the experiences of the City of Calgary planner who has worked within areas that exhibit the issues associated with problematic residential and industrial zone interfaces. The purpose of this interview is to:

1. Identify specific problems located at problematic interfaces
2. Record which strategies were employed, if any, in attempting to improve conditions at the problematic interfaces

The interview questions written before the interview were:

1. In what areas of Calgary have you been directly involved in addressing residential-industrial interface issues?
2. How did you tackle these issues? What solutions did you propose?
3. At what stage in the process did you enter (problem identifier or mediator)?
4. Who initiated the process?
5. What recommendations or possible solutions were proposed or adopted?
6. Did the actual policy solution mirror the original concepts?
7. How have the solutions succeeded?
8. How have the solutions failed?

The interview will not take more than 30 minutes. A copy of the consent form will be given to the participant.

Appendix P

Interview Transcripts

Interview with Tim Creelman

The interview questions written before the interview were:

1. **In what areas of Calgary have you been directly involved in addressing residential-industrial interface issues?**

Ramsay

2. **How did you tackle these issues? What solutions did you propose?**

The interface issues in Ramsay came about in the ARP process. Other issues, including the proximity of the Stampede grounds and concerns associated with the presence of the Stampede were of greater importance at the onset of the process. However, the interface issues grew in importance as the process unfolded. More important than the quality of the interface was the traffic into and out of industrial areas embedded in the community and the use and propagation of signage.

Tim proposed stabilizing the residential area of the community through design guidelines and capitalizing on the community status as the oldest community in Calgary by attempting to preserve as much of the historical character of the community as possible.

3. **At what stage in the process did you enter (problem identifier or mediator)?**

Tim carried through the entire process from its onset. The process took over 2 years, with the time waiting for approval taking the process to a three-year time span.

4. **Who initiated the process?**

The process was initiated through the usual steps. The issues in the community grew to a significant level of importance that the community and alderman asked that an ARP be prepared, and the community was deemed an appropriate place for an ARP to be written.

5. **What recommendations or possible solutions were proposed or adopted?**

According to the guidelines of the Municipal plan of the time, attempts were made at intensifying the community. The CPAC wanted the problems addressed concerning the Stampede and the high impact industry to the south.

6. Did the actual policy solution mirror the original concepts?

Ramsay was stabilized but did not become the site of intensification at a scale envisioned in the plan.

7. How have the solutions succeeded?

The industrial interface issue received a great deal of attention in the ARP because the Dominion Bridge industrial operation took a vested interest in dealing with the community. An employee of Dominion Bridge was a member of the CPAC.

The plan succeeded at having some land between the community and Stampede zoned PE from A (Agriculture).

Finally, a great success of the plan was the removal of all I-3 land use designations from the plan boundaries, and the insertion of lower intensity I-2 uses into these areas.

8. How have the solutions failed?

The attempt to intensify the neighbourhood was unsuccessful. A large area of residential land was to be rezoned as RM-2 or RM-4 near the industry at 6 St and Spiller Road.
A strip of land next to the rezoned PE land separating the Stampede from the community remained in the possession of the Stampede.

11 St was envisioned as a main street on a similar scale to 9 Av in Inglewood. This situation has not occurred as the area has gone to more of a warehouse, lower scale industrial/commercial use.

Interview with Philip Dack

How did the ARP remedy the residential-industrial interface issues in Inglewood?

1. The ARP calls for the creation of cost-sharing programme fund with industries. $10 000 was made available through the road department for tree planting. The money would be supplied upon redevelopment of industrial properties. This programme has yet to be initiated.

2. Three smaller industrial operations in the area were moved with monetary incentives supplied by the federal Neighbourhood Improvement Programme (NIP).

What particular problems fuelled complaints?

1. Certain smells from the distillery and yeast plant would reach homes to the east in windy conditions.

2. Industrial workers often work shift work and they would drive to work at all times of day. These trips would often go through residential streets. Also, delivery vehicles would uses these roads as 24-hour access points to the businesses.

The conversation turned to the specific issues faced at the former Petro-Canada refinery site.

- The site is so contaminated that the city or Petro-Canada would rather not have had responsibility for the area. The city eventually took on management of the site at no financial purchase cost.

- Houses along the western edge of the refinery were moved to other areas in Ramsay because of the pollution levels.

The impact of the CPR on the evolution of the area was mentioned.

The CPR, as an entity that predates the city itself, may have the ability to expropriate city lands in the area. The CPR acts as a quasi level of government and still has a tremendous degree of power in the region. The CPR, if challenged, may have the ability to supercede the LUB.

Philip suggests two possible strategies for older industrial sites:

1. Government buyout and relocation of sites.

2. Clean up and redesignation of sites.

Other successes of the ARP include:

- Getting rid of all industrial uses north of 9th Avenue. Only a remnant of industry remains at the old Sears warehouse.

- Philip referred to this ARP as a situation where planning actually made a difference.

- The key was not to attach new regulations, but to REMOVE certain regulations that were not allowing the area to redevelop according to the opportunities available. Certain regulations were in place that kept redevelopment form occurring, including:

    1. Setbacks along 9th Av. The draconian setback rules were relaxed for some development.

    2. AVPA rules changed. City council was petitioned to allow residential development within the 30-35 NEF airport sound contour in Inglewood. Council approved, and the provincial cabinet changed the regulation for Inglewood.

    3. Floodway rules weren't necessarily altered, but the current Inglewood Village site was raised 3 metres to put it above the floodplain. This addition of topsoil also put the site within pollution regulations and made it "non-polluted".

Appendices

Other comments:

- Redevelopment is risky at pollution sites, but if no pollution is registered, a site should be redeveloped.
- Sites of pollution can be bought and money placed into a redevelopment fund. This fund could be in the form of a municipal/provincial fund to later clean and redevelop the site, or, the private sector could be encouraged to clean and develop the site with a tax break incentive.

Criteria should be developed for buyout of industrial land:

1. No pollution on-site.

2. The redevelopment of the site should be supported by citywide policy.

3. A time frame for cleanup and redevelopment should be established.

4. Tax incentives for private developer or a city fund should be established early in the process with a clear goal of redevelopment.

Possibilities for New Policy

MAJOR INTERVENTION	MINOR INTERVENTION	NO INTERVENTION
-buyout	-land use policy tools	-leave the site as is
-acquisition criteria		
-redesignation of land		

Interview with Jim Francisco

Jim and I met to discuss the residential industrial interfaces issue. I knew that Jim had done some work on the Greenview area through correspondence last summer.

Firstly, Jim mentioned the North Bow Design Brief as the document containing policy concerning a tree-planting program to be conducted in the area. The trees were never planted along 1st Av NE. The interface at 1st Av NE is still in rough condition because the local residential property owners were unwilling to provide resources for the Local Improvement By-Law.

Jim's 2 ideas for providing a quick fix for the area were:

1. Planting trees as a screen (not approved by parks because of the low probability of tree survival). Malcolm Ho-You would be the contact to discuss the probability of tree planting activity being allocated to the area.

2. Screening by placing plastic strips in chain link fences.

The quick fix achieved was repairing the interior roads. This seemed sufficient for the local business owners.

A possible long-term solution is the creation of an Industrial BRZ. Because the Greenview area is a significant employment area (~3000 employed), the BRZ would improve the leveraging power of the local businesses. Jim mentioned that the Nisku industrial area in Edmonton might have adopted an Industrial BRZ.

There is a need in Calgary for a competing vision to the existing I-2 LUD for less intensive and smaller scale industrial uses that do not require high levels of planning intervention (expansive setbacks, soft landscaping, etc.).

Alderman Hawkesworth is interested in creating a Business Association of some kind in the area to mobilize the local interests. However, the maverick nature of the independent businessmen makes this difficult. The local businessmen continue to squabble about many issues, including parking. Also, there is reluctance to create a BRZ, or even quasi-BRZ organization because of the perception of what BRZs create, which seems inappropriate for industry (street furniture, sidewalk improvements, banners, etc.).

A committee was formed when Jim did his work in the area in 1998 and the results of this are the road improvements. Parking problems remain of paramount importance. Cars are parked all over the area, including illegally on boulevards and setbacks. The cars tend to destroy the peripheral land around the businesses.

There are policy possibilities for this area:

1. Create a new Industrial LUD, I2-A, designed for smaller parcel industrial uses

2. A blanket DC that would apply to the entire areas. The DC could address the urban design guidelines, setbacks, landscaping, and parking

A rethinking of the land use in the area is appropriate as available small lot industrial sites are lost to non-industrial uses, like the Sunset drive-in site being redeveloped as a church site.

Major interface problems include:

1. Parking along residential streets (1st Av NE)
   - A major violator is the bus company
   - Most sites have historical side deals struck with City agencies that make it difficult to control the issue with by-law or maintain parking standards across the area

2. Noise

3. Light pollution

Appendices

4. Traffic- interestingly, improving the quality of 1ˢᵗ Av NE may make it a more popular choice for heavy trucks, creating more traffic problems

5. Other Pollution (fumes, liquids, etc.)

The area as a whole tends to be filled with a wide range of low intensity industrial uses that are dependent upon customers living in the surrounding area. The area functions as a local industrial service area.

The business association would act to coordinate instigating simple improvement measures, including tree planting, screening, and parking.

A last ditch effort would be to encourage the local businesses to address the parking issues or be introduced to the friendly neighbourhood By-Law officer.

Interview with Diane Hooper

The interview questions written before the interview were:

1. **In what areas of Calgary have you been directly involved in addressing residential-industrial interface issues?**

Fairview

2. **How did you tackle these issues? What solutions did you propose?**

Diane's initial concept was to go through a land use redesignation process on the industrial side of the interface.

3. **At what stage in the process did you enter (problem identifier or mediator)?**

The Fairview mediation file has been passed along to a host of various planners over the years. Diane ended up with the file at the onset of her time with the City. At the end of the mediation process, it was clear there was no opportunity to solve the issues between residents and industry through mediation. Diane abolished the mediation committee and created a land use committee.

4. **Who initiated the process?**

The Fairview mediation process dates back to the 1970s, if not earlier. The problems associated with the interface have been in place since the area was built out in the 1950s.

5. **What recommendations or possible solutions were proposed or adopted?**

Diane suggested that land in the industrial area be redesignated to limit the scope of industrial uses allowed in the interface area. The new use zone would not be a DC zone, but would be a

146

new industrial interface zone that could be used in other interface areas in the City. The new zone would act to eventually phase out existing noxious uses as they were sold or moved from the area through the adoption of strict performance controls. Immediate shorter term solution included the placing of fencing or soft landscaping (hedges and trees) and augmenting operational traffic solutions, including barring loading and unloading in the alley.

6. Did the actual policy solution mirror the original concepts?

Eventually, the department decided that a land use study would be completed in the area. The study recommendations did not necessarily reflect the stricter tone of the original solution.

7. How have the solutions succeeded?

The mediation and then land use committee process succeeded in bringing people to the bargaining table.

8. How have the solutions failed?

The issues along the Fairview interface have existed for so long that the animosity between industrial owners and residents is pervasive. Industry business owners are not interested in finding a solution. The business owners would never accept Diane's solutions; remediation is a perceived threat to their property value.

Ultimately, the planner is caught in the political game. The planner has no power to enact a solution with any teeth, and the politicians are unwilling to take a stand as to anger as few constituents as possible. What the people of Fairview have been left with is a process that is without a planning solution since the construction of the interface in the 1950s.

Interview with Jack Scissons

Tim Creelman wrote the Ramsay ARP and did some work on a live-work project in an old industrial building in the area. Talk to him.

The interview questions written before the interview were:

1. In what areas of Calgary have you been directly involved in addressing residential-industrial interface issues?

a) Forest Lawn
b) Millican-Ogden (Ogden)
c) Manchester

2. How did you tackle these issues? What solutions did you propose?

The interface issues were raised in all 3 of these communities as part of an ARP process.

Appendices

a) The industrial component in the Forest Lawn area (Hub Oil and western Steel) was faced with complaints launched by the adjacent residents. Industry was contacted later in the process and the relationship between residents and industry was confrontational.
b) In Ogden, problems arose with smells emanating from adjacent offensive neighbour industries (including from the Alberta Processing Plant, which manufactured animal feed from animal carcasses). This process was less confrontational as concerned members of the community discussed the importance of the Plant with family members. It so turned out that the industrial neighbours employed a significant portion of the community and funded community enterprises.
c) The Manchester process went much more smoothly because all players were invited into review sessions at the onset of the process. In Ogden, there was little control or ability to influence business outside of the study area. However, because all players were involved early and the problems associated with the interface were included inside the study area, the plan succeeded. The industry and residents could learn about each other through establishing a dialogue.

3. At what stage in the process did you enter (problem identifier or mediator)?

In each area, Jack entered the process as the city planner, entrusted to find a land use solution through the ARP process.

4. Who initiated the process?

Each process was initiated through the standard community directed process, whereby community members perceive a problem or issue, address them to their alderman, who in turn recognizes a significant amount of issues were present to direct planners to create an ARP.

5. What recommendations or possible solutions were proposed or adopted?

a) A futuristic business/industrial plan was drawn up for Forest Lawn. The plan would involve an intensive tree planting and sign building program. This would serve as an enhancement plan for the area. With the 1980 LUB rewrite, I-2 was opened up as a retail and commercial district as well as an industrial district. There came to be inappropriate commercial uses in industrial designed areas (poor sidewalks, insufficient lighting, etc.) However, Jack viewed the move to retail in I-2 as a potential catalyst for the survival of older stagnant industrial areas. After a struggle, commercial uses remained in I-2 and remain a viable alternative for the reinvigoration of this underdeveloped industrial area.
c) Manchester was already undergoing a conversion to office use from I-2 before the Manchester ARP was written due to the area's prime central location.

6. Did the actual policy solution mirror the original concepts?

The Business Park was scrapped in Forest Lawn due to industry reluctance (the potential for high costs). However, the Manchester ARP solution remains as initially proposed.

7. How have the solutions succeeded?

The most successful solution in looking at residential-industrial interfaces is conducting noise studies. Richard Patchie will do a noise study for approximately half the cost of other consultants.
b) The Ogden south hill study cost between $8000 and $12000. Three noise metres were set up at different locations and collected readings for 3 days.
c) The Manchester noise study took place at 15 sites over 24 hours, at a cost of $5000.

The noise studies not only satisfied the CPC mandate for the studies to occur, but also provided the evidence that the residential uses on south hill could coexist with adjacent industry.

Behind noise studies, in terms of level of success, transportation studies are necessary to show movement pattern impacts on study areas.

8. How have the solutions failed?

Jack, as the consummate optimist, states that there is nothing that hasn't worked; recommendations just take time. For example, both Hub Oil and Western Steel were virtually untouchable at their locations. As nonconforming land uses, they were untouchable land uses even though they were massive violators of environmental and other policy. Both industries never updated their technology, which contributed to their downfall. Hub Oil eventually exploded in a dramatic fire and the site remains undevelopable, and Western Steel shut down instead of dealing with the discovery of high levels of lead poisoning in 15 workers.

Contamination has been minimal off-site at Hub Oil and Western Steel because of the low water table and heavy clay content of the soil.

Jack's Ultimate Recommendation- A buffer is required between I-2 and Residential space, be it open space or office parks (look at the Riverbend office park).

Other Thoughts
- Talk to Paul Batistella about his live/work development in Ramsay
- Look at the DC live/work development in Ogden in the form of townhouses behind the Texas T bar
- Determine what buffer strip width is appropriate between residential and industrial land uses. Jack proposes a ½ mile wide strip of "clean" industrial uses. It will be important to determine which uses are clean and not clean. Providing this buffer, in the form of a new zone, will:
    - Save lives
    - Avoid city liability problems

Appendices

Appendix Q

Forest Lawn-Forest Heights/Hubalta ARP Industrial Interface Policies

- **Industrial Policies** (Policy 1.6.3.b) will identify 48 St SE as the industrial-residential boundary to discourage industrial intrusions into residential areas.

- **Vision of the Community** (Policy 2.3) mentions, local industries will be upgraded and modernized to eliminate the noise and smells from polluting the surrounding residential neighborhoods.

- The primary goal of the ARP is to stabilize and revitalize the community. The ARP recognizes seven ways this goal will be achieved, three of which pertain directly to industrial interfaces, including:

    - ensuring that commercial and industrial development is compatible with adjacent land uses
    - discouraging commercial and industrial uses that give the community a poor image
    - enhancing the health and quality of life for all residents by addressing noise, odours, and traffic which impact the residential area

- **Industrial Land Use** policies are specifically addressed in section 3.3.

    - The **Context** section identifies the major industrial-related concerns to be addressed in the ARP, including:

        - the lack of maintenance of private property and screening of outside storage areas
        - truck traffic from the industrial area utilizing residential streets to access 17 Av SE
        - the oil recycling plant (Hub Oil Ltd.) and the steel recycling plant (Western Steel Ltd.) have been impacting the surrounding residential communities with objectionable odours, noise, and visual impacts.
        - The major goal is now to stabilize and visually improve this business/industrial area.

    - The **Objectives** of the ARP industrial land use section are to revitalize this business/industrial area by:

        - establishing a residential/industrial boundary that would discourage industrial intrusions into the residential area
        - improving the compatibility of Hub Oil Ltd. and Western Steel Ltd. with the surrounding residential neighbourhoods

    - The **Policies** of the ARP concerning industrial land use are outlined below.

- The [industrial] area should be recognized as a mixed use business/industrial park. A special DC District permitting a broad range of commercial and industrial uses is appropriate.
- The following uses are appropriate uses in this industrial/business area: autobody and paint shops; automotive sales and rentals; automobile services; automotive specialties; bottle return depots; ... kennels; laboratories; manufacturing, fabricating, processing, assembly, disassembly, production of packaging materials, goods or products; mechanical reproduction and printing establishments; ...signs.
- Uses that cannot meet the landscaping and screening guidelines should only be given temporary permits for two years. Site improvements should meet the minimum bylaw requirements within three years of their first-use approval.

- The **Development Guidelines** include regulations for landscaping and, state that all boulevards and front yards for new developments should be landscaped. Also, the ARP recommends the following varieties of trees for the area: elm, Colorado spruce, pine, Siberian larch, and bur oak.

- The **Residential/Industrial Business Boundary** is to be established at 48 St SE between 19 Av and Hubalta Rd, the east-west lane between 47 and 48 Streets, and the north-south lane between 17 and 19 Avenues. Businesses or industrial uses should not be allowed to the west or north of the boundary.

- **Parking** is addressed as follows. For sites abutting residential districts, the parking requirements of the Land Use Bylaw should be maintained.

- The **Circulations** section identifies that all discretionary use development permit and land use amendment applications for uses identified by the Calgary Police Service (CPS) as associated with criminal activity should be circulated to the CPS, the International Avenue BRZ office, and the community association for their comments.

- The **Industrial and Commercial Use** mentions that where potential soil and/or groundwater contamination from past and current industrial and commercial uses exists, appropriate remedial action should be taken to the satisfaction of Alberta Environmental Protection and Calgary Health Services.

Appendix R

Inglewood ARP Industrial Interface Policies

- The **Summary** section of the ARP includes a **Residential Recommendation** that calls for the funding of a cost sharing program with area industries to buffer residential areas from adjacent industrial development through fence construction, tree planting, etc. Such a program should be designed to cost the city no more than $10 000 per year and to be reviewed in five years. The city would contribute 50% of the cost of any improvements.

- The **Goals of the Inglewood ARP** relevant to industrial interfaces are:

    - To create, where necessary, and enforce laws controlling all forms of pollution so that industrial activity will be compatible with other activities in the community.
    - To encourage the relocation of industries if they fail to conform to required pollution regulations, and to replace such industries with a mixture of uses suitable to the activities, scale and character of the existing neighbourhood.

- Specific **Issues** acting to the detriment of Inglewood's health and safety are outlined:

    - The Petro-Canada Refinery Site and the CPR operations are blighting influences on existing and potential residential developments
    - The CPR yard and other industries cause various environmental impacts.

- A secondary objective of the **Residential Land Use** section is to improve the interface between residential and non-industrial activities.

- The **Industrial Development** section of the ARP identifies **Issues and Existing Conditions** facing the industrial areas. Many of the remaining Inglewood industries have a commercial or service component, which benefits from the central location of the community or are dependent on their proximity to the CP yards. Also, the remaining industries and the CP yards, although generally accepted by the residents as important to the community, still impose substantial negative impacts on the residential portion of the community.

- The **Objectives and Policies** of the Industrial Development section state:

    - the amount of land available for industrial development close to housing within the community should be reduced, no new heavy industrial development should be permitted within the community, and no new industry should be allowed along 9 Avenue or north of 17 Avenue.
    - the impact of industrial development on the residential portions of the community should be minimized. Monitoring of inappropriately located industries which may have negative environmental impacts (such as the tank welding shop) should occur and methods be developed to reduce the impact.

- The ARP recommends the **Residential-Industrial Interface** be addressed in four ways.

a) Redesignation of industrial land to require higher standards in new industrial development or to prohibit new industrial uses is proposed
b) Establishment of a limited financial program to encourage upgrading/screening of the industrial interface is recommended
c) Consideration of new legislation to achieve upgrading of vacant industrial sites adjacent to housing is proposed. New municipal legislative approaches are necessary if sites are to be rehabilitated to a reasonable standard while awaiting development
d) Community action is encouraged.

- **Industrial Pollution** is addressed by mentioning that Inglewood and some other residential communities have co-existed with industrial development since their founding. The relationship has often been positive with the industries providing employment for area residents. However, the ARP recognizes the negative impact of industrial activity, and mentions industrial sites, including the former Petro-Canada site and the Sears-Russel Steel site, by name.

- The **Residential Impact** of industrial pollution is addressed. The ARP states that:
  - there are a number of industries in Inglewood and adjacent communities which have substantial "nuisance" impacts on the residents. These problems most often arise from odours but may also be caused by glare, truck traffic and noise. In most cases these industries predate the Land Use By-law and are not subject to its provisions.
  - the appropriateness of taking action to address such interface problems has led to much debate. In some cases the industrial use was in operation prior to the residential development, in other cases there is a fear of loss of employment should overly onerous clean up conditions force an industry to close. The ARP does not recommend any specific action for such industries but does propose that the City identifies all such industries and determine what actions can be taken to reduce the impacts on the neighbouring residents.

- The **Recommendations** for addressing the residential impact include that the Industrial and Commercial sites task Force is directed to identify industries having substantial negative impacts on residential development. Each industry will be evaluated as to the severity and nature of the impact and the following factors will be examined:

  a) Possible mitigation measures and corresponding financial and other costs
  b) Short and long term development plans
  c) Alternate methods to encourage/require the industry to reduce impacts. This evaluation will be undertaken with the involvement of the owner wherever possible.

Appendix S

Manchester ARP Industrial Interface Policies

- In summary, the ARP recommends:

    - the development of a portion of the community with medium to high density residential that can be protected from traffic noise on MacLeod Trail and buffered from industrial impacts
    - the development of another section of the older Manchester residential community with local commercial and live-work, where impacts from the industrial area are currently unpredictable
    - no land use policy change in the industrial area

- The **Overall Goals** of the ARP include:

    - establishing a vital residential community with local commercial uses that are compatible with the existing adjacent general light industrial uses
    - protecting existing industrial uses from residential encroachment

- The **Residential Land Use** section calls for the retention of residential land uses within the community. The objectives are:

    - to minimize the impacts of traffic noise and industrial noise on the residential community
    - to improve the interface between residential and industrial uses

    The relevant **Policy** is that new residential developments should meet the Calgary Noise Bylaw regulations for outdoor amenity space and indoor spaces given the proximity of traffic noise form MacLeod Trail and industrial noise.

- In the **Commercial Land Use** section, commercial land uses are suggested as appropriate buffers between industrial and residential land uses. While in the past residential development across the lane from existing industry has been considered acceptable, it is not recommended in Manchester because it cannot be protected from the noise and other industrial impacts. The ARP recognizes the long-term possibility for change in the areas by stating that the long term policy for these blocks may change to allow residential if the existing industrial uses are replaced with uses that are more compatible with residential. An **Objective** of this commercial land use policy is to prevent residential uses encroaching upon adjacent industrial areas.

- **Local Commercial and Live Work Policies** include a provision for live work development. Live work does not allow outside storage, autobody, auto repair, paint, and welding shops. Businesses that involve the storage of propane, flammable or combustible liquids are prohibited. Nuisances including noise, odour, smoke, bright lights or anything of an offensive or objectionable nature, which is detectable to normal sensory perception outside the building, would be prohibited.

- The Industrial Land Use section of the ARP recognizes that a general light industrial and limited commercial policy is proposed for those sites utilizing the I-2 land use designation

Appendices

Appendix T

Millican-Ogden ARP Industrial Interface Polices

- The ARP calls for **Live-Work** land use to be designated along Ogden Road between the residential area and the Ogden shops. This district would allow small-scale business owners/residents to live and work on the properties. This district would allow...50% of the total floor area of the dwelling to be used for business purposes. The district would not allow medical clinics, veterinary clinics, retail sales, outside storage, autobody, auto repair, paint or welding shops. The live-work area includes the performance standard regulations proposed for Manchester, with the addition of the prohibition of uses producing electronic interference and dust.

- The ARP also recognizes that the existing and future residents will be subject to impacts from noise, dust, and light pollution from adjacent heavy industries. **Policies** concerning the South Hill industrial interface include:

    - While the South Hill mobile home park is located adjacent to heavy industrial uses, it is protected from noise and dust pollution by its location in an area with an elevation of approximately 16 metres below these existing industrial uses. In addition, during an independent noise study carried out by the City, noise levels in this lower area met the residential guidelines in Calgary's Noise Bylaw.
    - The plan recommends general light industrial uses, such as warehousing and storage, as a buffer between the Caravan Mobile Home Park and the heavy industries to the east and Glenmore Tr to the north. The location of these industrial uses will mitigate the noise and traffic impacts from the CP Rail and heavy industries to the east. The problem of noise is addressed in the ARP. An independent noise consultant has advised that if buildings in this general light industrial area are located close together and of sufficient height (5 metres) to function as a noise wall, the existing Caravan Mobile Home Park could meet the residential guideline in Calgary's Noise Bylaw.
    - The Approving Authority will encourage that the storage, vehicle parking area and exhaust fans in the industrial area be located away from the residential areas where possible.

- The **Industrial Land Use** section addresses only two small industrial areas at the north and south of the community, and does not address the interface with the Ogden Shops. The industrial policies include:

    - addressing the impacts and possible contamination of existing and past industrial uses on adjacent residential uses.
    - ensuring that these industrial sites are maintained and operated in such a manner as to avoid impacting adjoining residential sites with noise, dust, and/or vapour emissions.

- The Implementation of the Industrial Land use policy includes recognizing that the City of Calgary should establish a committee comprised of staff from various City Departments, community residents and affected property-owners to work with Alberta Environmental

Protection to monitor and ensure the effectiveness of ongoing reclamation activities at identified contamination sites.

Appendix U

Millican-Ogden CRP Non-Statutory Interface Policies

- **Summary of Key Issues to be Addressed** (Policy 2.2.1)- *Environment & Community Appearance* Complaints concerning vapour emissions from the Alberta Processing Plant; noise from the CP Rail and the two pipe processing plants (Ipsco Inc. and Prudential Steel); noxious smells from the former contaminated oil refinery lands; and the poor image of businesses, residences and the industrial area along Ogden Road.

- **Plan in Summary** (Policy 3.1.2)
    - Plant trees on the east side of Ogden Road between 50 Av and the CPR parking lots
    - Landscape and fence the CPR parking lot on Ogden Rd north of 69 Av
    - Encourage development of "live & work" type mixed land uses along Ogden Rd between 24 St to 74 Av SE. Up to 50% of the total floor area of the dwelling unit could be used for business purposes. Prohibited businesses include: medical clinics, veterinary clinics, retail sales, outside storage, autobody, auto repair, paint or welding shops, propane flammable or combustible liquid storage, producers of electronic interference, dust, noise, odour, smoke, bright lights, etc.
    - Address the negative impacts of the noxious smells and noise from the surrounding industries in the area

- **Tree Planting** (Policy 3.2.9.1.1)
    - *Goal-* To screen the industrial plants and parking areas, to enhance the visually neglected parts of the neighbourhood, and to ensure that Millican-Ogden continues to be a well-treed community.
    - *Action Plans-* It is recommended that the Environment Committee:
        - work with representatives from the Calgary Parks and Recreation department, private industry and various government agencies to determine the most appropriate tree pruning and planting projects for their community
        - encourage local industries and businesses to donate trees for neighbourhood enhancement and promote involvement of local industries and businesses in the planning and implementation of park planning and tree planting projects.

- **Noise and Clean Air** (3.2.9.1.1)
    - *Goals-* To address the industrial impacts of noise and vapour emissions in order to improve the air quality in Millican-Ogden while at the same time ensuring the viability of these industrial operations both now and in the future.
    - *Action Plans-* It is recommended that the Environment Committee:
        - encourage continued involvement of the local industries in dealing with the clean air and air quality issues in Millican-Ogden
        - promote communication with the representatives of the local industries; encourage their involvement in the processing of mitigation programs; and discuss the feasibility of joint-venture agreements for a cooperative undertaking of the environmental improvement projects

- **Contaminated Properties** (Policy 3.2.9.1)
    - *Goal-* To ensure proper rezoning for any action or redevelopment of a property that is found to be contaminated.

Appendix V

Ramsay ARP Industrial Interface Policy

- The ARP objective concerning **Industrial Land Use** is to address the impacts of existing and future industrial development on adjacent residential areas.

- The **Context** section of the Industrial Land Use section states that:
    - the 1974 Ramsay Design Brief sought to improve the industrial/residential interface with measures including land use redesignations and truck zone and route removal.
    - The Environmental Protection and Enhancement Act and regulations enforce strict controls on industrial land use with respect to pollution and reclamation, as well as more pervasive liability requirements.
    - The I-3 land use classification, allowing the heaviest and most intensive industrial development, is generally thought to be incompatible with the adjacent residential community...alight industrial and commercial designation is appropriate.
    - It is essential for a liveable residential environment that traffic and other impacts from major uses be addressed so as not to adversely affect these areas.

- Industrial Land Use **Policies** include:
    - A general light industrial policy is considered appropriate. DC (I-2) areas are proposed, as well as eliminating the existing I-3 heavy industrial land use designations, to accommodate industrial and commercial uses that have minimal impact on adjacent residential areas.
    - In the event of a major development proposal for large portions of the vacant industrial lands, a concept and site plan shall be submitted addressing the interface with adjacent residential areas. e.g. berming, landscape buffers, setbacks.

- The Industrial Land Use section of the ARP concludes with an implementation section listing recommended Development Guidelines and Proposed Actions to be employed at 3 different industrial areas along the residential interface. Policies pertaining to industrial site 1 are included below.
    - The intent of the Development Guidelines is to permit the development of a range of light industrial and commercial uses compatible with an adjacent residential community; provide a land use concept plan framework so that when industrial and commercial development does re-occur it will do so in a way that does not substantially impact adjacent residential uses.

- Perimeter Interface Area Development Guidelines include:
    - No shadowing should be permitted by proposed developments to extend beyond the opposite curb line along Spiller Road and 24 Av SE adjacent to the perimeter interface at noon on September 21.

- Stepped-back building facades are encouraged to reduce the visual mass and shadowing.
- As the perimeter interface area develops, building design should reference the character of the existing original [industrial] structures.

• The following guidelines are also to be encouraged:

- where the site abuts residential uses, landscaping should include soft landscaping to the satisfaction of the Approving Authority
- the original [industrial] buildings should be adapted and re-used for new light industrial and commercial uses in order to preserve and enhance these examples of early industrial architecture in Calgary.

• The Proposed Action for the Perimeter Interface Area is to provide a transition of height and use intensity between residential areas and industrial operations at the interface area.

References

Alberta, Government of. Municipal Government Act. Calgary: Alberta Queen's Printer. 2002.

Ale, B.J.M. "Dealing with Risk in Environmental Policy in the Netherlands," Acted du symposium "Gerer les risques industriels" organise par le Conseil canadien des accidents industriels majeurs et l'Ordre des ingenieurs du Quebec. Montreal: Sept. 24-25, 1992.

Barnett, Jonathon. The Elusive City; Five Centuries of Design, Ambition, and Miscalculation. New York: Harper and Row Publishers, 1986.

Calgary, City of. Bowness Area Redevelopment Plan. Calgary: City, Community, and Downtown Planning Division. Dec., 1995.

Calgary, City of. Calgary's Land Use Bylaw Phase 1 Report. Calgary: Land Use section, Development and Land Use Division. Feb., 1979.

Calgary, City of. City of Calgary Task Force on Industrial and Commercial Sites report to the SPC on Operations and Environment. Calgary Nov. 4, 1991.

Calgary, City of. Community Association Maps, 2001. On-line.
    Available: gov.calgary.ab.ca/planning/land_use_planning/community_profiles/index

Calgary, City of. Fairview Land Use Study Land Use Options Report (Draft). Calgary: Planning and Transportation Policy, March 2002.

Calgary, City of. Forest Lawn-Forest Heights/Hubalta Area Redevelopment Plan. Calgary: Planning and Building Department. Nov., 1995.

Calgary, City of. Inglewood Area Redevelopment Plan. Calgary: Planning and Building Department. May, 1993.

Calgary, City of. Low Density Residential Housing Guidelines for Established Communities. Calgary: Planning and Building Department. May 1993.

Calgary, City of. Manchester Area Redevelopment Plan (Proposed). Calgary: Land Use Planning Division. April, 2002.

Calgary, City of. Millican-Ogden Community Revitalization Plan. Calgary: Planning and Building Department and Community and social Services Department. Dec., 1999.

Calgary, City of. Noise By-law, 1995. On-line.
    Available: gov.calgary.ab.ca/community_standards/relevant_bylaws/noise

References

Calgary, City of. North Bow Design Brief. Calgary: The City of Calgary Planning Department. March, 1977.

Calgary, City of. Ramsay Area Redevelopment Plan. Calgary: City and Community Planning Division. Sept., 1994.

Calgary, City of. "Report of Town Planner, Thomas Mawson," in The City of Calgary Past, Present, and Future. Calgary: City of Calgary Planning Commission, 1914.

Calgary, City of. Report on the Status of Disaster Preparedness in the City of Calgary. Calgary: Calgary Disaster Services Committee. Dec. 8, 1999.

Calgary, City of. Short-Term Growth Management Strategy-Industrial 2000-2004. Calgary: Planning and Building Department, June 2001.

Calgary, City of. The Calgary Plan Municipal Development Plan. Calgary: City of Calgary, July 20, 1998.

Calgary, City of. The City of Calgary Land Use By-law 2P80. Calgary: Land Use section, Development and Land Use Division, Mar. 31, 1980.

Calgary Tribune. "Windborne Scents Prevail Over Calgary," Calgary Tribune. Dec. 1886.

Carlston, Jason. Letter to the author. May 14, 2002.

Cormier, Ray. Communities of Calgary: From Scattered Town to a Major City. Calgary: Calgary Century Publications, 1975.

Creelman, Tim. Personal Interview. June 12, 2002.

Dack, Philip. Personal Interview. July 5, 2002.

Davidson, Michael. "This House is an Office: Residential-Office Districts", Zoning News of American Planning Association. Oct., 2000.

Edmonton, City of. Edmonton Noise Bylaw No. 7255. Edmonton: City of Edmonton, Dec. 14, 1994.

Edmonton, City of. Edmonton Zoning Bylaw 12800. Edmonton: City of Edmonton, 2001.

Edmonton, City of. Plan Edmonton: Edmonton's Municipal Development Plan. Edmonton: City of Edmonton, Aug. 31, 1998.

Edmonton, City of. Summary Review of Zoning Techniques. Edmonton: City of Edmonton, Oct. 15, 1995.

Farr, Adam. "Performance Based Zoning for Industrial Land", <u>AACIP Planning Digest.</u> vol. 5 #3, 2001.

Farr, Adam. "Performance Based Zoning for Industrial Land, part II", <u>AACIP Planning Digest.</u> vol. 6 #1, 2002.

Foran, Max. <u>Calgary, An Illustrated History.</u> Toronto: James Lorimer and Co. Pub., 1978.

Foran, Max. "Early Calgary, 1875-1895: The Controversy Surrounding the Townsite Location and the direction of Town Expansion," in <u>Cities in the West: Papers of the Western Canada Urban History Conference.</u> A.R. McCormack and Ian MacPherson, editors. Ottawa: 1975.

Francisco, Jim. Personal Interview. May 15, 2002.

Great Britain, Statutes of. <u>The British North America Act, 1867.</u> Adopted March 29, 1867 as the Statutes of Great Britain (1867), 30 & 31, Victoria, ch. 3.

Gray, James. <u>The Roar of the Twenties.</u> Toronto: 1975.

Haar, Charles. <u>Land Use Planning: A Casebook on the Use, Misuse, and Re-use of Urban Land.</u> Toronto: Little, Brown, and Company, 1959.

Hamilton, City of. <u>Hamilton Zoning By-law #6593.</u> Hamilton: City of Hamilton, 1980.

Hodge, Gerald. <u>Planning Canadian Communities; An Introduction to the Principles, Practice, and Participants.</u> Scarborough: Nelson Canada, 1991.

Hooper, Diane. Personal Interview. June 11, 2002.

Laux, Frederick A. <u>Planning Law and Practice in Alberta.</u> Edmonton: Juriliber. 2002.

Levin, Earl, "Zoning in Canada," <u>Plan Canada.</u> vol. 7, June 1957.

Logan, Thomas H. "The Americanization of German Zoning," <u>Journal of the American Institute of Planners.</u> vol. 42, Oct., 1976.

Merriam-Webster. <u>Collegiate Dictionary.</u> 2002. On-line. Available: m-w.com/cgi-bin/dictionary.

MIACC (Major Industrial Accidents Council of Canada). <u>Risk Assessment Guidelines for Municipalities and Industries; An Initial Screening Tool.</u> Ottawa: MIACC, Oct. 1997.

MIACC (Major Industrial Accidents Council of Canada). <u>Risk-Based Land Use Planning Guidelines.</u> Ottawa: MIACC, 1995.

References

Nasmith, Catherine. "Toronto's Niagara Neighbourhood: Re-Integrating Industrial and Residential Uses", Viewpoints. Jan.-Feb. 1994.

North Riverside, Illinois. "Steady-State Vibration Limits Standards" in Schwab, Jim. Industrial Performance Standards for a New Century. APA, Planning Advisory Service Report 444, March 1993.

OECD. Guiding Principles for Chemical Accident Prevention, Preparedness, and Response. Environmental Monograph no. 51. OECD: 1992.

Ottawa, City of. Ottawa Official Plan. Ottawa: City of Ottawa, 1994.

Ottawa-Carlton, Regional Municipality of. Region of Ottawa-Carlton Official Plan. Ottawa-Carlton: RMOC, April 1999.

Ottawa-Hull. Ottawa-Hull 1915 Plan. Ottawa-Hull, 1915.

Regina, City of. Regina Development Plan. Regina: City of Regina, 2002.

Regina, City of. Regina Zoning By-law No. 9250. Regina: City of Regina, June 29, 1992.

Saskatoon, City of. Industrial Land Inventory. Saskatoon: City Planning Branch, Community Services Department, Aug., 2001.

Saskatoon, City of. Municipal Enterprise Zones. Discussion Paper, 2002.

Saskatoon, City of. Saskatoon Development Plan Bylaw No. 7799. Saskatoon: City of Saskatoon, 1998.

Saskatoon, City of. Saskatoon Zoning Bylaw No. 6772. Saskatoon: City of Saskatoon, 1987.

Schwab, Jim. Industrial Performance Standards for a New Century. APA, Planning Advisory Service Report 444, March 1993.

Scissons, Jack. Personal Interview. June 6, 2002.

Toronto, City of. 1904 Toronto Building By-Law. Toronto: City of Toronto, 1904.

Toronto, City of. Toronto Official Plan Part 1. Toronto: City of Toronto, 1987.

Toronto, City of. Toronto Official Plan Summary. Toronto: City of Toronto, 2002.

Van Der Ryn, Sim, and Cowan, Stuart. Ecological Design. Washington, D.C.: Island Press, 1996.

Vancouver, City of. CityPlan. Vancouver: City of Vancouver, 1995.

Vancouver, City of. Zoning and Development Bylaw No. 3575. Vancouver: City of Vancouver, 2002.

Victoria, City of. Victoria Official Regional Plan. Victoria: City of Victoria, 1974.

Victoria, City of. Victoria Zoning Bylaw. 1998.

Winnipeg, City of. Plan Winnipeg. Winnipeg: City of Winnipeg, 2001.

Winnipeg, City of. 2002 Zoning Bylaw Summary. On-line.
    Available: city.winnipeg.mb.ca/ppd/zoning.stm

Wissenschaftlicher Buchverlag bietet

kostenfreie

Publikation

von

wissenschaftlichen Arbeiten

Diplomarbeiten, Magisterarbeiten, Master und Bachelor Theses
sowie Dissertationen, Habilitationen und wissenschaftliche Monographien

Sie verfügen über eine wissenschaftliche Abschlußarbeit zu aktuellen oder zeitlosen Fragestellungen, die hohen inhaltlichen und formalen Ansprüchen genügt, und haben **Interesse an einer honorarvergüteten Publikation**?

Dann senden Sie bitte erste Informationen über Ihre Arbeit per Email an info@vdm-verlag.de. Unser Außenlektorat meldet sich umgehend bei Ihnen.

VDM Verlag Dr. Müller Aktiengesellschaft & Co. KG
Dudweiler Landstraße 125a
D - 66123 Saarbrücken

www.vdm-verlag.de